Don't Call Me Marky Mark

Don't Call Me Marky Mark

THE UNAUTHORIZED BIOGRAPHY OF MARK WAHLBERG

Frank Sanello

RENAISSANCE BOOKS
Los Angeles

ALSO BY FRANK SANELLO

Cruise: The Unauthorized Biography (1995)

Spielberg: The Man, the Movies, the Mythology (1996)

Naked Instinct:
The Unauthorized Biography of Sharon Stone (1997)

Jimmy Stewart: A Wonderful Life (1997)

Eddie Murphy: The Life and Times
of a Comic on the Edge (1997)

Stallone: A Rocky Life (1998)

Library of Congress Cataloging-in-Publication Data
Sanello, Frank.
Don't call me Marky Mark : the unauthorized biography of
Mark Wahlberg / Frank Sanello.
p. cm.
"Filmography/Videography/Discography": p.
Includes bibliographical references (p.) and index.
ISBN 1-58063-071-5 (trade paper : alk. paper)
1. Marky Mark, 1971- . 2. Rap musicians—United States—
Biography. I. Title.
ML420.M3312S26 1999
791.43'028'092—dc21
[B] 99-10090
CIP

10 9 8 7 6 5 4 3 2 1

Design by Hespenheide Design

Distributed by St. Martin's Press
Manufactured in the United States of America
First Edition

For my four-legged family,
Marshmallow, Lucrezia, Cesare, and Catullus,
the only "people" I allow to wear fur.

ACKNOWLEDGMENTS

Academy of Motion Picture Arts and Sciences (Margaret Herrick Library), Kris Andersson, Michael Anketell, Arabours, Joey Berlin, Dr. Dan Berrios, Dr. Daniel Bowers, Louis Chunovic, Bill Crawford, Ernest Cunningham, Ivor Davis, Anita Edson, Alan Effron, Cyrus Godfrey, Interscope Records, David Izenman, Professor Benjamin Sifuentes Jauregui, Richard Johnson, Gary Kirkland, Amanda Kragten, Dr. David Krefetz, Rod Lurie, Christina Madej, Paul Manchester, Donald J. Myers, Fr. Joe O'Brien, Sia Prospero, Linda Reinle, Doris Romeo, Marjorie Rothstein, Professor Anthony Sabedra, Catherine Seipp, Guy Shalem, SoundScan, VideoScan, Dr. Brent Walta, and Jeff Yarbrough.

I also wish to thank my agents, Mike Hamilburg and Dorie Simmonds, and my editor, James Robert Parish, for his invaluable assistance in researching and crafting this work.

CONTENTS

I wanna dedicate this book to my dick.

—from rap star Marky Mark's 1992 autobiography

I'm very spiritual. I communicate with God.

—Mark Wahlberg, actor, 1997

INTRODUCTION

What Makes Marky Run?

That's why I always think I've got a horseshoe up my ass.

—Mark Wahlberg, 1998, attributing his career to dumb luck

The rap star formerly known as Marky Mark has changed more than his name in the last few years. Not since Cher evolved from a Bob Mackie fashion joke into an Oscar-winning actress has a Hollywood performer engineered such a dramatic career makeover.

But instead of Cher's feathered G-strings and disfiguring tattoos, Mark Wahlberg's original image was even wilder. The hazel-eyed hunk became a nationally known figure by dropping his pants at the end of a concert performance in 1992. The decision to strip hadn't been choreographed or planned. The beyond-buffed star simply pulled down his pants on the spur of the moment.

Later he became a supermodel for underwear emperor Calvin Klein and had his photographed pose first unveiled on a ten-story-high billboard in Times Square. Nothing came between him and his Calvins except millions of grateful voyeurs. Thereafter, Wahlberg continued his walk on the wild side when he allegedly bashed gays and Madonna, two "special-interest groups" you don't want to get on the wrong side of.

Only twenty-seven, Wahlberg has had more reincarnations than Shirley MacLaine: street thug; ex-con; platinum-selling rap star; billboard beefcake, a muscle god bestriding Times Square in cotton undershorts instead of toga; respected A-list actor sought after by Robert De Niro and Oliver Stone.

Unlike other young movie stars of recent years such as Charlie Sheen and Brad Pitt, who do endless variations on their greatest hits, Wahlberg doesn't play it safe. His films are most startling *not* because of their outrageous themes that range from porn to heroin addiction, but for the sheer diversity of subject matter. He's played a junkie and a grifter, a lame-brain G.I. and a codependent hit man. This is not Tom Cruise endlessly replaying the callow young man who gets religion by film's end. (Start with 1983's *Risky Business* and continue on to 1996's *Jerry Maguire*.)

Even the porno world of 1997's *Boogie Nights*, Wahlberg's most out-there movie subject to date, didn't push the envelope far enough for the actor. For a while, he had signed on to star in *8mm* (1999), which explores an even more subterranean area of moviemaking and flesh-peddling—snuff films. (For the uninitiated, snuff films are porno with a twist. According to urban legend, the performer is supposedly "snuffed"—i.e., killed—at the climax!) However, wiser minds, most notably Wahlberg's, prevailed, and the actor eventually dropped out of *8mm*, leaving the role to Oscar-winner Nicolas Cage, who is an even bigger risk-taker artistically.

The actor's large following, including a sizable number of gays, will turn out for anything the buffed Bostonian does careerwise. On-screen or off-, the southpaw from South Boston is an object of intense interest and awe. People can't keep their eyes off Wahlberg. When he works out at Gold's Gym in Hollywood (the pumping ground of fifteen-minute phenomena like Fabio and Lucky Vannos, the construction worker in Diet Coke commercials), gymgoers suddenly lose their cool, despite daily sightings of other celebs like Jodie Foster and Magic Johnson. Between sets, gym members gape at Wahlberg like unabashed tourists.

Wahlberg-watching at Gold's is fun—like an indoor sport, except the spectators don't cheer, they just sneak a peek. He brings so much baggage with him—plus entourage and wardrobe—that gawking at the superstar is more than your typical fan playing peek-a-boo.

Something's going on. And a few mutual friends have told me their theories.

In January 1998, I was using the incline bench press at Gold's when Wahlberg appeared with two buddies to do the same exercise on a piece of equipment next to mine. The coincidence—biographer and subject doing the same pump at the same time and place—seemed karmic. (Also great primary research for me.)

After a quarter century in the trenches of celebrity journalism, to say I am no longer starstruck is not just an understatement; a more accurate term might be "star-overloaded." One reason for my jadedness is that more than likely I've already had lunch or brunch with the star and then had to go home and write 2,000 words sheepishly promoting his/her latest film/TV show/haircare/lip gloss project/product.

My indifference disappeared when I saw Wahlberg in person at Gold's in 1998. I had noticed him before at the gym and was struck by the apparent sadness in his handsome face. Also by his baggy lumberjack shirt which hid a taut body that in magazines looks as though it was ripped from the pages of Michelangelo's sketchbooks. But in early 1998, something was different about Wahlberg from my previous sightings of him at the gym. The lumberjack shirt had been traded in for an even baggier sweatshirt and sweatpants. He also had embryonic whiskers which made him look even younger than his then twenty-six years. And he had gained a *lot* of weight.

.n fact reminded me of another wunderkind who'd ɪe scales before his time—Orson Welles. Mark's eyes half-obscured by puffy cheeks. A few days later, a ɪ.. ɪ me out of the blue and said without prompting, "Did you see Marky Mark at the gym? He *has* gotten tubby, hasn't he?"

An actor and colleague of the star told me Mark had put on thirty pounds for a new film, *The Corruptor*, which began filming in Toronto in March 1998. In the noirish drama, he plays a homicide detective, the typical overworked cop who doesn't have time to hit the gym but apparently hits the donut shop too often. My source, also a close friend of the actor, said, "They paid him $2.5 million for that film. I'd put on weight for $2.5 million." The source, a superfit actor, added, "I've seen his abs. He's got no abs. His waistline is *fat*. He has love handles."

To bulk up for the role, the source said, Mark imitated Robert De Niro in *Raging Bull* (1980), stuffing himself with junk food. Wahlberg's four-bedroom, fourth-floor penthouse apartment on Doheny Avenue just south of the Sunset Strip and the exclusive Hollywood Hills, looks like "product placement for Hostess snacks" in a movie, another visitor to Mark's home told me. "It's decorated in Early Twinkies, So Ho Ho-Ho's!"

Another mutual acquaintance told me, "He's got a stackload of donuts, cookies, and pastries at his house stocked up all the time!"

While some bods-to-die-for at the gym snickered at Wahlberg's Delta Burke-ish bod, others praised him for sacrificing his physique for his art. A man who had made his name and fortune largely on his physical appearance had willingly trashed that image for the greater good—a movie role. When Method actor De Niro bulks up for a movie project, no one giggles or pokes a finger in his gut. Sylvester Stallone was similarly praised when he traded his abs for a paunch in 1997's *Cop Land*—and earned the best reviews of his screen career. Meryl Streep starved herself on a diet of white wine and little else, to play a Holocaust survivor and won an Oscar for *Sophie's Choice* (1982). Not since Sharon Stone went without washing her hair for two weeks or wearing designer gowns to play a gritty cowgirl in *The Quick and the Dead* (1995), has an actor famous for physical perfection been willing to trash himself for a movie role. "It's all about the work," not the workout, another actor once said, about subordinating himself to the demands of the script.

The junk food which fueled Mark's physical transformation, like everything else in his penthouse, is neatly arranged. Mark is a very tidy, neat person, friends say. His place is minimally furnished and doesn't look "lived-in." Four bachelors live there, but the penthouse is anything but a classic "bachelor's pad." There are lots of "grown-up" toys like video games, a big-screen TV, a pool table, and a state-of-the-art stereo system, but the boys in the penthouse seem to be all business and no play. Instead of a 1990s version of the Playboy mansion, with starlets falling out of their bikinis and all over the master of his domain, the Wahlberg residence more resembles a library's reading room than a hangout for young studs and their young squeezes. "Mostly, they just sit around and read scripts," a frequent guest there told me.

While Mark's apartment may look more like a monastery than a swinger's digs, he doesn't lead a monklike existence. Although one mutual acquaintance told me Wahlberg didn't date much because he's "so focused on his career," another said that sometimes he pursues women, especially at the gym.

A friend of eight years who works at Gold's described Mark's method of operation inside and outside the weight room. "He sees me training beautiful women, models, actresses. He's always asking me, 'Hey, you gotta hook me up. You gotta introduce me to her!'" The close associate, who asked to remain anonymous, tells Wahlberg to introduce himself, but the actor persists and wears his friend down. "So when I *do* try to set him up, he puts on this fake persona of, he's Mr. Shy Guy, and I know he's not. He's *not* Mr. Shy Guy."

Wahlberg seems to have a gentler version of Dr. Jekyll-Mr. Hyde's dual personality. At the gym, he's passive—a beta male. On the street, he's all alpha, a young Warren Beatty with an even better bod. His longtime pal says, "When we're outside the gym, he'll go up to a girl and say, 'Hey, baby! How ya doing, baby? My name's Mark Wahlberg, and I think you're very beautiful! I think we should go out tonight.'"

This friend adds with amazed amusement, "I cannot believe that works! Sometimes it does. I tell him, 'Why are you [doing this]? "Hello" would be nice.' But that's his way. It's weird. He can be like that outside the gym, but inside, when I try to introduce him to girls, he's quiet. I don't know. You tell me what that might be about."

Director Penny Marshall confirms that outside the gym Mark isn't standoffish. She described one memorable trip in Los Angeles with Wahlberg, who appeared in her film, *Renaissance Man* (1994): "Mark was riding in a car, and he rolled down the window and said to the girls in the next car, 'Can you help me with directions?' And they said, 'Where to?' And he said, 'Your house.' That's *very* Mark."

Despite his status as a star of screen and billboards, with a body one national magazine described as "abdominally intimidating," Mark doesn't always get the girl in real life. And the reason, a friend says, revolves around the only thing Mark actually feels insecure about.

A mutual pal told me the handsome actor can be cocky, but when he is, "I put him in his place. I know what will hurt him as far as his emotions." Insisting on anonymity, the friend says Wahlberg is insecure about his height, which has been reported in various magazines and books as ranging from five feet four inches (!) (*Playgirl*), to five feet nine inches (his biographer, Randi Reisfeld, author of *Marky Mark and the Funky Bunch*, 1992). One publication described Wahlberg as "physically imposing . . . despite a height deficit." When I saw the actor at our gym, he appeared to be roughly my height, five feet nine inches.

His slightly-below-average stature has hurt him in the romance department at least once, according to a friend. "A really beautiful girl I knew—I know her very well, she talks to me a lot"—caught Mark's interest and he asked for an introduction. "You gotta hook me up with that," Wahlberg said, pointing in her direction. When the pal tried to play matchmaker, the beautiful woman, a statuesque five feet eleven inches, said, "Who, *him*? I think he's really cute, but he's way too short for me. I prefer tall guys."

The friend asked one of Mark's roommates if he should relay the woman's response to the star. The roomie strongly discouraged him, saying it would hurt Mark's feelings. When Mark persisted in learning her reaction, his friend lied and said, "She'll meet you." "I didn't tell him the truth," he admitted.

Officially, however, Mark pokes fun at his height. Lynn Goldsmith, who co-wrote his 1992 autobiography, *Marky Mark*, once asked him, "When you started playing basketball, you were pretty small. Were other people bigger than you?" His response: "Other people are *still* bigger than me." The photo that illustrates this quote in his autobiography speaks volumes about what an overachiever Mark is and how he has compensated for literal and figurative shortcomings to achieve his current stature in the entertainment industry. The picture shows Mark playing basketball with friends who are indeed taller. However, his head is way above the crowd because he's about three feet off the ground. The camera catches him suspended in air.

Another friend who has also been to Wahlberg's West Hollywood penthouse believes the junk food and the dramatic weight gain have less to do with Wahlberg's professional needs and more to do with his recreational habits. The source, who has known Wahlberg for several years as a business colleague and personal friend, told this author, at the French Market in West Hollywood, California, on February 18, 1996, "Mark has the munchies because he gets stoned seventy to eighty percent of the time . . . during the day too!" This buddy, who hangs with the penthouse-mates, has personally seen the gang light up marijuana cigarettes. One of the four young men who share the penthouse with Wahlberg, "is stoned all the time," according to this eyewitness.

A successful actor himself, the pal has urged Wahlberg to lay off the marijuana because it will eventually stall his career and dull the focus which has put him near the top of the A-list of actors. "I said, 'Hey, instead of a positive impact, it will probably have a negative impact!'" the friend told me. Marijuana may indeed have a positive effect as a sedative, but no one has ever stayed at the top of his form stoned out of his mind. Look what marijuana has done for the careers of Cheech and Chong.

How did Mark respond to this "Just say no" lecture? "He just kind of looked at me and smiled. What can you do?" the pal said, shrugging his shoulders sadly.

Another good friend who used to hang out at Mark's bachelor pad when he had a house in the Hollywood Hills before relocating to the penthouse in 1997, says he never saw Wahlberg light up, but believed "marijuana smoking was happening. He seems pretty *altered*. He seems a little stoned sometimes."

The editor-in-chief of a major magazine recalls a four-day photo shoot for a cover story on Mark. A newly minted superstar, Wahlberg was still feeling his way along the corridors of fame and public obsession. The editor hypothesized that Mark was nervous about the shoot and to relax, smoked marijuana nonstop. "He really smoked *a ton* of pot," the editor told me in a phone interview in April 1998. "He was really high. I'm pretty familiar with that kind of high." Indeed the editor was. Both he and the reporter who did the cover interview smoked along with Wahlberg and his handlers, although the journalists claim they didn't partake as much. "It was amazing how much he smoked and how much the guys around him smoked and were constantly passing joints to and fro," recalled the editor, now a major TV producer.

The editor, who has been covering celebrities for fifteen years, theorized that for Mark, pot was nothing more than a way to unwind. "He was perfectly functional, yet smoking constantly. Whatever he was smoking was probably keeping him relaxed and taking the edge off a potentially stressful situation. He was very nervous about the cover shoot and the interview. He seemed so shy."

Months later, on the day I shared the gym floor with him at Gold's, Mark didn't seem shy. Even more shocking than his physical transformation was the icy expression on his face. The depression I had noticed on previous occasions was gone; anger had taken its place. Mark Wahlberg looked pissed. A good friend suggested that marijuana was a way to relax, let go of the anger, although the friend didn't know the source of Mark's emotions. Another source and mutual friend suggested Mark's use of marijuana was a way to self-medicate, and agreed with my observation that Mark appeared depressed when I saw him at the gym. "I don't think he's very happy. If someone was truly happy they wouldn't do what he does to himself . . . smoking [marijuana] all the time." The associate speculated the depression arose from a need to constantly improve himself, whether it was to add more muscle to his body, or better film credits to his résumé. "I just think he wants more for himself. He's never satisfied."

Maybe Mark was having second thoughts about the wisdom of trading in his abs of death for love handles. He is on the record as someone who cares greatly about his physical appearance. Eight years earlier, at perhaps his studliest, Mark was already worrying about losing his bod and obsessing about his absence from the gym during a hectic concert tour. A visitor to his hotel room in Jackson, Mississippi, reported that the twenty-year-old rap star looked in the mirror and hated what he saw. "I got to get to the gym, man. My shit is melting!"

The day I saw him at Gold's, his anger was scary, even though he didn't say a word to the other club members, strenuously trying to pretend they weren't—like me—following his every move. Mark didn't hassle anyone, but his presence was intimidating. If there is such a thing as passive-aggressive weightlifting, that's what the star seemed to be doing.

It didn't help that Wahlberg had brought along two even-scarier-looking dudes, who share Mark's penthouse. One is a boxer, Mark Basile, thirtyish, with a rose tattoo on his right deltoid and a killer left hook. (I know. I've seen him assault the "banana bag" on the second floor of Gold's.) Basile is an aspiring actor with cable-TV credits like *The Red Shoes Diaries*. He is also Wahlberg's occasional trainer and constant traveling companion, who accompanies his pal and employer to every movie set. A mutual friend of the two Marks says Basile has "pretty much given up his [acting] career, basically, and lives on Mark's shirttails. Mark [Basile] has been nothing but a great friend. He's a great person. He's very spiritual. I think that's why Mark [Wahlberg] keeps him around."

Two sources said that none of the young men who shared Wahlberg's house in the Hollywood Hills or the penthouse pays rent. To make Basile feel as though he's paying his way, Wahlberg uses him as a personal trainer, even though he already has one in Los Angeles. Wahlberg also gives "Basile a couple thousand dollars here and there to pay his bills. Mark is very generous," a close pal of Basile's told me. In fact, almost everyone I interviewed for this book has mentioned Wahlberg's generosity, which is unconditional. He has helped friends and even acquaintances get auditions and jobs that would have been impossible without a gentle word to the powerful from their benefactor. "He helps *everybody*," his friend and trainer, Sia Prospero, told me, "and he doesn't ask for anything in return."

When I saw Mark and his crew of two at Gold's, Mark's other workout partner seemed even more intimidating than boxer Basile; that is, until I took a closer look. This bud looked like a gang member. Shaved head. Tattoos. Baggy togs straight from the barrio. Or so it seemed. I was only two feet away from the trio and realized a more accurate term for him was "gangbanger wannabe." Both his shirt and pants sported the Calvin Klein label—designer duds for imitation thugs. As the late comedian Fred Allen said, "Once you strip away all the phony tinsel in Hollywood . . . you find the *real* tinsel!"

Wahlberg's two-man entourage, which is actually one too many guys for an efficient workout, was also notable for more than the visuals. None of them spoke to one another—and certainly not to the lookey-loos pumping in the vicinity. Wordlessly and with no coordination, weights were lifted, plates added to the load. No grunts, no groans. Of course, autograph-seekers need not apply—and they didn't.

Wahlberg's depression-turned-anger at the gym intrigued me. I had already begun researching this book when I caught him supine on the incline bench, but at the time I didn't have a clue as to what really makes Mark tick.

I spent months and thousands of words trying to find out the answer to that intriguing question.

—Frank Sanello, West Hollywood, California

CHAPTER 1

Anglo Barrio

Anything I put my mind to, I can't sleep till I accomplish it.

—Mark Wahlberg, 1997

The Dorchester section of Boston is the kind of neighborhood you want to be *from,* not *in*. Twenty minutes and three miles south of downtown Boston, it's the sort of place upwardly mobile blue-collar folks flee. This phenomenon even has a name, "white flight." Not a slum, but not *Leave It to Beaver*'s 'burb, either. Donna Reed's perfect sitcom mom would have broken out in hives if her husband lost his medical license and the family had to move to this Anglo barrio.

In a 1997 interview with Wahlberg, *Rolling Stone* described Dorchester in the early 1970s as "a place you'd never want your precious ones to grow up in." A prominent business executive, a Wharton MBA who works in Boston, offered me his take on Dorchester. "My impression of it is that it's very middle class/blue collar . . . bifurcated, half Irish, half black. Old housing stock, small lots. Dorchester is stable now, not declining. But it's not rapidly improving. Some 'boys' are moving in," the executive said, referring to the gay men who are contributing to the area's revitalization.

A professor of urban planning at Harvard felt the business executive was being kind or maybe owned property in the neighborhood and overstated its stability to drive up the value of his investment. The professor said, "Not much of Dorchester is gentrified except for small enclaves. It's one of the worst areas in Boston. Dorchester has some really tough areas." The Harvard professor thinks Dorchester is more depressed than Boston's even tougher Southie area.

In 1971, the year of Wahlberg's birth, the neighborhood was in even worse shape, the scholar says. "Dorchester was particularly depressed during his childhood." The Wahlbergs lived right off the street that gives the area its name. "Dorchester Avenue is the worst part. There are no single-family homes on the avenue," the professor insisted. Tongue in cheek, he added, "Dorchester is the equivalent of Brooklyn—*without* the nice parts!"

Today the neighborhood's melting-pot image seems ironic, since a quarter century earlier, when Mark was born, it was a more homogeneous stew. If the future star had been exposed to such a smorgasbord of racial and sexual diversity, his life might have taken a different turn.

Mark Robert Michael Wahlberg was born on June 5, 1971, at St. Margaret's Hospital in Brighton, twenty minutes away from Dorchester. He was baptized by Father William Walsh on August 1, 1971, at St. Margaret's in Dorchester.

Mark was the baby of the brood, number nine. With striking hazel eyes and a tuft of dark blond hair, Mark was doted on by his siblings. His prolific mother, Alma, had had six children from two previous marriages: Debbie, Arthur, Michelle, Paul, Jim, and Tracey. Wahlberg Senior and Alma produced Donnie Junior, Robert ("Bobbo," until he punched out anybody who called him that), and Mark.

Alma was a registered nurse who worked at a local hospital at night and "daylighted" as a bank teller. Donald Senior was a Teamster. He drove a truck and, later, a bus that delivered lunches to schools and hospitals. Leftovers from work often ended up on the Wahlberg dinner table. Mark and Donnie stacked dozens of single-serving milk cartons in the fridge and ate individually wrapped cookies. "We had lots of Oreos and school milks," Mark remarked years later, in dramatically different surroundings—his manager's New Jersey mansion. Early on, the youngsters learned to show social responsibility toward those even less fortunate than themselves. When the Wahlbergs had a surplus of school leftovers, the kids bicycled the remains of the day to even poorer families.

Mom and Dad's combined incomes, however, even with the free bus lunches, were not sufficient to keep nine hungry little Wahlbergs in Chee-tos and Kool-Aid. Both parents held down two jobs or more, at the same time, during Mark's childhood. Their meager financial gain was the family's spiritual loss. Without bitterness, Mark has said that he and his brothers were not supervised by their parents. That's an understatement. Alma admits poor parenting skills. "Emotionally, I just wasn't available to him," she has said.

Mom and Dad's four-plus jobs could only pay the rent on a tiny, three-bedroom apartment—part of a three-family row house on a steep, winding Dorchester street. The Wahlbergs lived on the first floor, with two more families stacked on top of them in a vertical triplex sliver.

The Victorian gingerbread structure was airy, with lots of windows and a balcony on each floor. However, even with all the ventilation and light, the Wahlberg residence was jammed. Do the math: That's eleven family members with only three rooms to lay their heads! Mark remembers sharing not only a bedroom, but the bed as well, with six brothers. Arthur was the oldest, followed in descending chronological order by Paul, Bob, Jim, Donnie, and the baby, Mark. Sandy, the family mutt, slept with the boys, and a pet generically named "Turtle" hid under the bed. Three hundred years earlier, New England's Puritans had called this dense sleeping arrangement "bundling." In the 1970s, it was just plain overcrowding. Interestingly—perhaps because he had never known anything else—Mark didn't find the cramped living arrangements invasive. For him, the physical closeness translated into an emotional connection. A sense of security remains his strongest childhood recollection. He told a biographer in 1992 that sharing a bedroom with five brothers and two pets "just seemed normal."

But close quarters often led to close encounters of the hostile kind. With all those budding male hormones confined in such a small space, dissension was bound to occur. And it did. "We were always very physical with each other, there was a lot of roughhousing and some pretty bad fights," Mark once said, without elaborating.

Donnie was more forthcoming about arguments that turned ultraviolent. Fortunately, Dad was even tougher than his kids. "One time we were having a fight and I was holding [Mark] by the shirt up near his neck and he was just punching away at me. I was trying not to punch him back," said Donnie, who has always looked out for his baby brother, even as an adult. "I don't know why this particular time I wouldn't punch him, because we'd punched each other before, we'd had crazy fights before. He was just swinging away, punching me about a hundred times in one minute. Finally I got fed up and punched him in the face! Right when I hit him, my father walked in the door and kicked my ass!"

At the Wahlberg home, these outbursts were more like a tribal rite of fraternal bonding than vicious sibling rivalry. After every set-to, the brothers would reaffirm their mutual affection. According to Donnie, "Whenever we had a serious fight when we were little, we'd talk, really open up and get in deep, and that's when we'd kiss each other. Now we do it all the time. Whenever I'm leaving Marky or he's going away, or like even when he finishes in the studio and is takin' off, we always kiss good-bye." Mark, on the other hand, has never mentioned this sibling "smooching." At twenty-one, he would say that his slugfests with Donnie were mostly a thing of the past. "Me and Donnie haven't had a fight in a long time, a real goin'-at-it, duke-'em-up fight. But I feel, yes, I will wax that ass if I have to."

At home, the boys fought each other; outside, it was the Six Musketeers against the world. One for all. All six for one. Other kids learned not to pick on one Wahlberg because five more would quickly come out swinging—or worse.

Dorchester, at the time, was not only ethnically but economically homogeneous as well. There were no rich kids living down the block to make Mark feel inferior. That was, until the Teamsters went on strike and Donald Senior had to get off the bus and join the picket lines. The patriarch of the family was a staunch union man. For him, scabbing wasn't an option—desperation was. For the first time in his early life, Mark felt ashamed to be poor. The rest of the children on the block didn't have money for extras, either, but when Donald went on strike, the Wahlbergs didn't have money for basic necessities. The box lunches ended when the strike began. The family suffered the ultimate working-class nightmare. They were reduced to relying on food stamps from the welfare department.

Years later, Mark was still traumatized by the retelling: "I used to be embarrassed as shit to go to the store with food stamps because all my friends would be there. I'd say, 'Dad, I don't want everybody knowin' we're on the food stamps.'" The strike eventually ended, and so did Mark's shame. This lean period, in fact, had a beneficial effect. It left him with a lifelong respect for money and a frugality that continues to this day, despite $2.5 million-per-film paydays and a penthouse near the pricey Hollywood Hills-Sunset Strip area of Los Angeles.

The Wahlbergs also found ways to make do with very little. Rich imaginations made up for a poor bank balance. Mark loved baseball and basketball, and excelled at both. He couldn't afford to go to professional sporting events, but he rarely missed a Red Sox, Celtics, Bruins, or Patriots game, thanks to the TV and radio.

The family couldn't afford to go the movies, either, so a highlight of the week was Sunday-night bingo games at home. The Wahlbergs, German-Irish Catholics, also attended fund-raising musicals at their place of worship, St. Gregory's Church, on Dorchester Avenue. Mrs. Wahlberg once had had aspirations of becoming a professional dancer, and she frequently appeared in the church's musicals. The rest of the family sat in the audience and cheered Alma on.

Back home, Dad supplied family entertainment of another sort. After a few beers, he would regale the kids with tall tales only the baby of the family seemed to accept as fact. "My father used to tell me how he lost his arm in the war and they sewed it back on. I'd go and tell all my friends, and my brother would be like, 'That ain't true, you shithead! Who told you that?' I said, 'Dad told me that.'" His brother would respond, "Yeah, that's 'cause he just drank a couple of Schlitzes and you kept bothering him to tell you something, so he gave you a story."

On Mrs. Wahlberg's rare days off from work, she'd cram as many kids into the car as she could fit, for a trip to the local beach. Mark remembered only one family vacation during his entire youth, a long drive to "sunny" Maine.

His parents did their best with what little they could save. Mark's sister Tracey got to take ballet lessons. One Halloween, Donnie and Mark—the future rappers—borrowed her dance outfits: a family-album snapshot shows the two guy in tutus! Mark almost never got any of the toys he saw advertised on TV, and as the baby of the family, his wardrobe invariably consisted of hand-me-downs. As an adult, he would be thrifty in his wardrobe purchases, preferring jeans or sweatpants to Armani and Manolos, except when Calvin Klein was literally paying him millions to hype haute couture.

Life in the Wahlberg triplex wasn't all Charles Dickens and outtakes from *Oliver Twist*, though. One Christmas, Mark's parents somehow managed to save up enough money to buy bicycles for all nine children, according to Randi Reisfeld's *Marky Mark and the Funky Bunch* (1992). A fond memory from Mark's childhood remains running down the stairs that Christmas morning and finding nine shiny new bikes arranged around the tree.

Although the Wahlbergs were devout Catholics, that didn't stop his parents from divorcing in 1982 when Mark was eleven.

A newly single parent, Alma Wahlberg now had even less time to supervise her children, especially the rambunctious boys. She blamed herself for the kids' drift into thuggery and worse. Mrs. Wahlberg said she was too busy working and feeling sorry for herself to scream at the kids, "Cut it out!"

She should have done a lot of screaming.

Within a year of the divorce, Mark began acting out. Like most children, he took his parents' split personally. Years later, he recalled his feelings at the time. "I was going berserk when it first happened. I thought, 'They *have* to live together because of me!' I realized afterward that if they couldn't be happy with each other, then they shouldn't be together."

His first act of rebellion didn't send him to reform school, but it left him literally permanently scarred. At twelve, the youth decided to take pride in his Irish heritage, and he self-tattooed a shamrock into his left leg with an unsterilized sewing needle and India ink. (That's the way they do it in prison, too.) Eerily, years later, in a film in which he played a handsome psycho, he would use the same technique to carve his girlfriend's name into his perfect torso. Except in the movie it was makeup, and fake. The shamrock was real and indelible. It also hurt like hell. Mark would later admit it was "a stupid thing to do," but that didn't stop him from adding to his human canvas over the years an entire gallery of body art, including a tattooed rosary around his neck. Ouch! Still a devout Catholic, he explained the tattoo as an act of devotion rather than self-mutilation. Years later, he had plastic surgery to get rid of the creepy shamrock tattoo, but still "wears" the rosary!

The tattoo and the pain made young Mark feel and look tough. He described his endurance of physical pain in a way that sounds more masochistic than macho. "I got bruises and scars all over my body. I got one on the inside of my knee from falling through a fire escape on the fifth floor—the stair was missing. I got scars all over just from bein' a wild little kid."

Mark was also, by his own admission, not a terrific student. While Donnie was an academic star, even something of a teacher's pet, Mark was more a classroom troublemaker. It was a mutual lack of admiration society between teachers and student. "I hated [school]. With a passion. I hate that shit. I made trouble."

But not the typical kind of trouble. He dealt with his hatred of school in a passive-aggressive away. Instead of acting out, he opted out. Mark Wahlberg became a truant. "I swear, I left home every day *meaning* to go to school . . . but I'd meet my posse in front, hang out, and then walk off, hit the stores. I was always down at the mall, hangin' out down the street or at the local pizza joint."

All the Wahlberg children attended the William Monroe Trotter School in Dorchester from kindergarten through the fifth grade, and it required a bus trip to reach the school on Humboldt Avenue. During the commute, Mark and his brothers made friends who would last a lifetime and play a pivotal role in their future careers. Donnie became good pals with one of the boys on the bus, Danny Wood, while Mark became an even better friend of Danny's younger sibling, Brett. Jordan Knight, the same age as Mark, rode the bus with his older brother Jonathan. Years later, the Knight brothers, Danny Wood, and Donnie, would form the pop group New Kids on the Block.

Although Jordan would later work with Donnie, it was Mark he bonded with, maybe because they were the same age. He had mixed feelings about Donnie at the time. "Everyone thinks I was close to Donnie when we were younger, but that isn't true," Jordan recalled in 1992. "Donnie used to bully me—in a good-natured way. He'd come over and squeeze my cheeks and say, 'Jordan, you are so-o-o-o cute.' It was Mark I was close to. We were good friends, and we used to hang out."

Mark corroborates the friendship, but his memories of the battles on the bus differ from Jordan's. The brothers Knight—Jordan and Jonathan—did the scuffling, not Donnie, who confined himself to the odd cheek-pinch. "Me and Jordan were in the same class, second, third, and fourth grade. I'll never forget how he and Jonathan used to fight on the bus!" Mark said.

A sign of things *not* to come occurred when the future members of New Kids on the Block tried out for Mrs. Rose Holland's glee club at the Trotter School. The Knight boys and Danny Wood made the cut. Mark, who years later would confess he couldn't sing, didn't make the singing team. More surprisingly, Donnie, who can sing and went on to a solo recording career after the New Kids, was also rejected by Mrs. Holland. Neither of the Wahlberg youngsters seemed to mind. There was always baseball or basketball to absorb their energy. Or the odd fistfight/wrestling match in their overcrowded sleeping quarters.

Maybe because Donnie and Mark were nearest in age to one another, the two boys were also tighter emotionally than they were with any of their other siblings. Their mom recalls, "My two youngest boys were always the closest. They were constant playmates, and sometimes wrestling partners."

Mark insisted these wrestling matches were fun rather than feuds, despite the ferocious-sounding "ring names" they adopted for their mat time. "We had nicknames during our fights. I was always 'the Crusher,' and he was 'Ling Choy,' the karate expert."

Donnie also fought with his elder sibling, Robert ("Bobbo"), in what sounds like an attempt to establish pecking order based on age. Almost two years older than Mark, Donnie has said, "Me and Bobbo fought a lot, and me and Mark fought a lot, 'cause we were right in that close age bracket. I wanted to show Bobbo that I was tough and old enough to hang with him and his friends, and Mark wanted to show me that *he* could hang with me and *my* friends. But the truth is, none of us could really hang. I couldn't deal with Bobbo, and Mark couldn't deal with me."

Although good-natured, the fights between Mark and Donnie represented something more than horseplay. They concealed a fierce sibling rivalry, where Mark always felt inferior to his older brother. Ironically, Mark's career would one day surpass Donnie's, as the latter's acting career became becalmed in the doldrums of TV movies, while Mark has become one of the most sought-after actors in Hollywood.

However, this is now. That was then: Donnie was the "star" of Dorchester Avenue. Mark was a supporting player who had trouble keeping up with his older brother, whom biographer Randi Reisfeld described as possessing "a special magnetism everyone was drawn to." It also didn't help that Donnie, unlike Mark, was an excellent student and immensely popular. Plus Donnie always got the girls during their adolescence.

Donnie also acted as "family therapist" when feelings in the overcrowded apartment got ruffled. His "counseling" even extended to the grown-ups. Alma would confess that she treated Donnie more like a confidant than a son. "He was my protector," she said, the child she turned to for her emotional needs. Donnie was solicitous about his baby brother's emotional life, as well. Donnie was, and is, a great guy to have as a brother. Friends recall Donnie praising Mark's athletic prowess and fixing him up with surplus girls, since Donnie had more than he could handle and was happy to share.

In Reisfeld's biography, Donnie modestly downplayed his own charisma and generosity toward a baby brother he always took care of. Looking back in 1992, at the age of twenty-three, Donnie reasoned his youthful magnetism was more the result of exhibitionism, his career drive nothing more than attention-getting. "I didn't have show-*biz* aspirations. I had show-*off* aspirations," Donnie said.

Long before he commandeered concert stages, Donnie held court in the family's living room, cracking jokes, performing self-penned songs, and providing more entertainment than the Wahlbergs' typical Sunday-night bingo in the cramped parlor. Donnie's specialty was impersonating singing idol Michael Jackson. He found a cheap version of Jackson's trademark jacket and single white glove at a thrift store, and learned to imitate the pop king's moonwalk and other signature moves. Donnie imitated Michael so well, the family encouraged him to enter local talent contests, which the boy with "show-off aspirations" happily agreed to do.

CHAPTER 2

Nouveaux Riches Kids on the Block

Donnie's decision to enter talent contests began as a lark and turned into a $100 million-grossing career as a pop star. At one local amateur performance, a well-connected woman caught Donnie's act and, like the Wahlberg family, was immediately impressed by his magnetism and charisma. The woman, identified only as "Gina" in a 1992 biography of Mark, happened to be the next-door neighbor of Mary Alford, an artist's manager in Boston who represented R&B star Rick James. In 1984, Alford was trying to create a white, pop version of the Jackson 5, teenagers as cute as a button who could be packaged into a stage and recording act that would appeal to teenage girls.

Gina told Alford about this terrific youngster who could do Michael Jackson better than Michael Jackson. "You've *got* to audition this kid named Donnie. He raps and he dances and he is so terrific." Gina carefully omitted what both Donnie and Mark would later concede about themselves: They can't really sing!

Alford began her search for the Great White Michael Jackson—Donnie Wahlberg, fifteen years old—in 1984. She had heard that Donnie and his pals hung out at Dorchester Park, right across the street from the Wahlberg triplex. However, when she went there, Donnie couldn't be found. Kids who were in the park gave Donnie's home address to Alford, and the intrepid manager tracked him down.

In the summer of 1984, Alford knocked on the Wahlbergs' door and invited Donnie to audition for a new pop group she and her partner, Maurice Starr, were packaging. At fifteen, Donnie didn't know Alford or her partner's track record. Starr was the producer of New Edition, then Boston's hottest teen singing group, with hit singles like "Candy Girl" (1983) and "Is This the End" (1983). Its members went on to fame as solo artists: Bobby Brown (the future husband of Whitney Houston); Johnny Gill; and the trio known as Bell Biv DeVoe (Ricky Bell, Michael "Biv" Bivins, and Ronnie DeVoe). Donnie actually blew off the woman who would make his career by saying he had to mow the lawn and invited her to return when he finished!

Alford wasn't put off so easily. She was tenacious, and returned after he finished cutting the grass. (It was a quick job. Pictures of the triplex show a tiny, postage-stamp-sized front yard that was more weed than grass.) Donnie recalls, "She did come back. She came back to take me to Maurice's for the audition. I went with Mark."

Alford hadn't heard about Mark and definitely hadn't invited Donnie's younger brother to tag along. As usual, Donnie was looking out for his baby bro. In fact, the two boys agreed that Alford would have to take them as a package or not at all.

Donnie went to the series of auditions with minimal expectations. Donnie knew his singing talents were modest at best. The amateur hours at home had been a distraction encouraged by the family. Fortunately, Alford and Starr weren't looking for the pop equivalent of Pavarotti. They wanted "cute," which sells records to young girls. "If an incredible singer had walked through the door, a really great singer, I don't think he'd have had any better chance than I did of making the group," Donnie later said, when he realized what the producers had really been after.

Maurice Starr was captivated by Donnie's stage magnetism. After only a handful of tryouts, he signed the youngster. At Donnie's insistence, Mark became group member number two, although even their adoring mother felt that it was only the wrapping, not the package, that had gotten Mark the gig. "They loved Mark! They just loved him. He was little and cute," Alma said in 1984, the summer her son turned thirteen.

It finally dawned on Starr that perhaps singing *talent* was an essential ingredient of a singing group. After signing the two boys, he sent them to not one, but two music coaches, paying for his new clients' lessons. Starr probably got favorable terms, since the music teachers were also Starr's brothers.

Meanwhile, Alford kept scouring the blocks of Boston for more potential New Kids on the Block. But before she found them, Donnie and Mark had already gone into Starr's home recording studio to cut a demo reel.

"Artistic differences," which would eventually blow up into a full-scale riot about what constituted "music," began almost immediately. After years of composing for the family living-room musicales, Donnie liked to write songs even more than he enjoyed imitating Michael Jackson's moonwalk. Mark collaborated on the compositions and found he loved the process more than the performance. "We even wrote a song together, a rap song, a whole song, just me and Mark," Donnie said. Mark seconded the emotion about the collaboration. "Me and Donnie wrote this rap and it was so cool. It was really what I was into at the time!"

It makes sense that both youngsters preferred rap, since it requires rhythmic speaking rather than actual singing. There was just one little problem. In 1984, white rap was nonexistent, and Starr wasn't interested in creating a vanilla version of black hip-hop.

While Mark and Donnie were pushing "gangsta" lyrics, Starr wanted what would turn out to be the New Kids' signature style, bubblegum music! Their future hits would include "I'll Be Loving You Forever" and "Cover Girl," not "Kill Da Poh-leece" or "Shoot Da B****!"

Donnie remembered Starr's initial reactions to their rap offering. "It started to turn around a bit, and Maurice would say, 'Okay, that's fine, now I want you guys to sing this ballad.'"

After a few months, Mark, only thirteen, would demonstrate the supreme self-confidence and self-possession that would later have him fighting powerful studio executives over scripts—and winning! Mark announced that he wanted *off* the Block. "I was feeling like I just didn't fit. They were starting to do more ballady stuff, and I just couldn't see myself singing 'I'll Be Loving You Forever.'" Not the kind of sentiment that would one day be expressed in such classic rap lyrics as "I shot the b**** upside the head!"

Or as Mark diplomatically put it, the group's music was "bubblegum shit!"

Wahlberg also had problems with the New Kids' emerging clean-cut image at a time when he wanted to present himself as one mean *mutha*. Blame it on puberty. Or good taste, which found "bubblegum" tough to chew. Like a maid who refuses to wash the windows, Mark had serious artistic reservations about the direction Starr was leading the then duo. "I don't do bubblegum! I'm a serious rap artist!" he explained.

One critic felt rap's subliterate lyrics and musicless music simply represented an alternate way of selling out. It was as commercialized and prepackaged as the studio-sweetened sound of bubblegum. Another critic said that rap, with its faux gangstas in designer ghetto/barriowear, was often more Madison Avenue than the Archies, the top "pop group" of the mid-1960s.

At thirteen, Mark turned his nose up at bubblegum. At twenty-one, still in tough-guy mode, he would continue to put down the New Kids and their old style of music. However, mellower and more humble at twenty-five, he finally offered a less self-serving reason for his exit. "'Was it hard to sing so bad?'" he asked rhetorically, about a scene in *Boogie Nights* where his porn-star character tries to launch a recording career. "It's not hard at all. A lot of mixing and effects went into my records, you know? The real trip about why I wasn't in the New Kids—why I 'quit' the New Kids—I actually got kicked out because I couldn't sing!" he told a London magazine in the early 1990s.

Then Wahlberg dropped a bomb in the interview that could have exploded the New Kids' music career, if the Kids hadn't already fragmented into solo acts. "New Kids On the Block," he told *The Independent*, "was mostly a lot of lip-synching anyway!" (A similar revelation destroyed the pop duo Milli Vanilli.)

Ultimately, the reason Mark left the New Kids standing on the block had more to do with a thirteen-year-old boy who just wanted to have fun, not a career. While Donnie was driven to become a star, Mark's fantasy lay more along the lines of hoop dreams—basketball, that is. Alma Wahlberg admitted that the baby of the family wasn't exactly career-obsessed at the dawn of his teen years. "I don't think Marky knew what he wanted for a while. He did dance, and he did some rap, but he really wasn't into it. He certainly wasn't as regimented as Donnie. He was more sports-oriented and kind of lackadaisical. While it was fun, it was okay, but when it got to be hard work, he left." (Years later, a born-again workaholic who made three movies per year, Mark agreed that at thirteen the only "drive" he had was down a basketball court. "I felt the group was taking up far too much of my time. I was young and I just wanted to be a kid.")

Typically, Donnie defended his brother and his career decision. Mom might have disparaged Mark as "lackadaisical," but as far as his older bro was concerned, "the kid [was] all right." "I respect him for not staying with the group," Donnie has said. "It took a lot for him to stand up and say, 'No, this is not what I want to do.' Because everyone was pressuring him to stay with it, telling him, 'You'll be rich, you'll do this, you'll do that, you'll be famous.' So for him to stand up and say no, that took a lot of strength and a lot of character, and I respect him for it. I hope he doesn't have any regrets."

Alford and Starr didn't regret Mark's decision, either, but they were becoming frantic for a more practical reason. Mark's departure left them with only one New Kid. In desperation, they turned to their Kid and asked, "Do *you* know anybody who might be interested in joining [this group of one]?" Indeed, Donnie knew several candidates, and he turned out to be as savvy at A&R as in catching the eye and ear of Alford and Starr.

Donnie suggested that his friends, the boys on the Trotter School bus, join New Kids on the Block: Danny Wood, Jonathan and Jordan Knight, and another friend, Jamie Kelly.

While Donnie helped out his young pals, his suggestion to hire them didn't immediately help his career. Their first single, "Be My Girl," came out in 1984 and promptly hit the remainder bins. However, New Kids on the Block and their managers didn't let this failure stop them from trying again—and succeeding. But it would take five long years.

Meanwhile, as a much better lyricist, John Lennon, once said, "Life is what happens to you while you're busy making other plans." A lot of life happened to Mark after he departed the band.

CHAPTER 3

Meanwhile, Back on the Real Block

In 1984, at age fourteen, Mark flunked his freshman year at Copley High in downtown Boston. He was forced to repeat a grade. Still touchy about the subject eight years later, he insisted that truancy, not stupidity, had held him back at Copley. "It wasn't that I was dumb," he said in 1992, "I just felt there was better stuff on the streets." During his second go-round in ninth grade, he showed up for class a total of ten times. Then at fifteen, in 1986, he dropped out of school for good. With no distracting classes to attend, Mark could devote himself full-time to getting into trouble.

Years later, in August 1997, Mark shared his daily routine at fifteen with a reporter from the *New York Times* for the paper's prestigious Sunday magazine. Wahlberg apparently hadn't shared this information with his mom at the time it was happening.

From the young man's "to do" list:

"Every day was: Wake up, go out, hustle, make money, steal, sell drugs, rob people, do drugs. By normal standards, I should have been locked away, and they should have thrown away the key."

Most "babies" of the family get special treatment and affection from parents and older siblings who treat them like, if not babies, little dolls or playthings. Not Wahlberg. "It was definitely hard being the last. By the time I was growing up, my parents had to have been exhausted, because I was running around in the streets all hours of the night, drugs in the house, money, coming up with new cars—all kinds of stuff. And nobody knew what was going on until I would have to make the phone call and say, 'I'm in jail.'"

Mark started out small, "doing runs," in his words (to one national magazine)—"shoplifting" in everybody else's. "Our family was very big, so we didn't have much money at all. I started stealing stuff. [I]f I saw something in a shop that I couldn't afford, I'd just try and steal it anyway."

Five-fingered bargains soon turned into having both hands in the till or sitting behind the wheel. According to Mark's own account, he robbed liquor stores and got away with grand-theft auto. However, it was probably more like "joyriding under the influence," a condition he seemed to be in a lot during these *deformative* years, as he referred to them. Beer and angel dust were his drugs of choice.

Wahlberg and his Celtic posse ambushed drunken Irish construction workers as they stumbled out of neighborhood bars in Dorchester with what was left of their Friday paychecks. Thoughtfully, they waited for the working stiffs to pass out before rolling them. Then they would empty their marks' pockets and "rip wedding rings off their fingers," Wahlberg said in an October 30, 1997, interview with Erik Hedegaard in *Rolling Stone* magazine.

Overworked, Mrs. Wahlberg blamed herself for her wild child's antisocial behavior. "I wasn't aware that he was going wrong, and I should have been. If I wasn't preoccupied with my divorce and all that stuff. . ." she said.

Alma never did grab the baby of the family by his "cute" cheeks, as she described them, and drag him to school. Mrs. Wahlberg was busy raising a houseful of kids on her own, and she didn't have time to feed her brood, let alone check out the neighbors' refrigerators, before rushing out to one of her two jobs. If she had, her son's biggest nightmare might never have occurred.

In 1988, sixteen-year-old Mark and his pals were rummaging through a friend's freezer to defrost some food for dinner. Instead, he found himself thawing out what, years later, he would euphemistically call "wacky tobacky." Substance-abuse counselors call it PCP, "angel dust," or elephant tranquilizer, which is PCP's "prescribed" use.

Wahlberg says the elephant dope was the stash of a friend's mom. His account: "I went into my friend's mother's freezer and found something I thought was a bag of joints, we smoked it, and it was wacky tobacky and we went crazy," he told *Interview* magazine in October 1997.

PCP turns most people into zombies. If it can knock out a five-ton pachyderm, imagine the effect on the motor skills of human inhalants. (Typically, PCP comes in liquid form. Users dip cigarillos in the stuff and smoke them for a synergistic high of tobacco and the drug that can bring Dumbo to his knees.) Mark's reaction to the drug was atypical. After a puff or two of the powerful sedative, most people become near-comatose and a threat to no one or nothing but their beating heart, which can go into cardiac arrest. For a handful of PCP users, however, the drug has an amphetamine-like effect, increasing their energy and giving them superhuman strength. At the same time, the anesthetic component of PCP makes its users immune to physical pain.

Rage may have been what Mark and his buds experienced after they smoked the neighbor's frozen "TV dinner" and then engaged in what sounds like outtakes from the TV series *Cops.*

Post-PCP, the liquor stores were unfortunately closed, and Wahlberg needed a drink. He spotted an Asian man on the street and demanded his beer. The man demurred, and Mark beat it out of him with a five-foot-long, three-inch-thick wooden pole, leaving his victim for dead.

Taken into police custody, Wahlberg remained unrepentant. Court documents reveal he "made numerous unsolicited statements about gooks and slant-eyed gooks." Another report said he called the Asian man a "Vietnam fucking shit!"

According to the police, this was not the youth's first demonstration of political incorrectness. Two years prior to the assault and battery for the sake of a quick beer, Mark had chased black schoolgirls, screaming racial epithets as they ran, their bookbags flapping in the breeze. *New Times,* a weekly alternative newspaper in Los Angeles, reported in an October 30, 1997, article that Wahlberg and the other white boys in the 'hood didn't restrict themselves to hurling racial invective. They threw rocks at the girls, who were returning from the beach. *New Times* unearthed Massachusetts court records that claimed Wahlberg and other youths on bicycles (!) chased the grade-schoolers, shouting, "Kill the niggers! Kill the niggers!"

The bicycle attack went unpunished. The assault on the Asian man in 1988 was not dismissed. Examining the youth's previous infractions, the Boston district attorney began to see a pattern. The prosecutor called the beer-mugging "racially motivated," and Mark was charged with attempted murder. The charges were eventually reduced to assault and battery.

The judge gave Mark a choice, which Wahlberg may have felt was more like "pick your poison": As a juvenile, he could accept a lesser charge and remain in a center for wayward youths until the age of eighteen. The nightmarish alternative: Plead guilty as an adult (at sixteen!) and serve only six months. However, he would have to do his time in the state penitentiary in Plymouth, fifty miles southeast of Boston.

Mark tried to look tough on the day he was sentenced. "My mom gave me her cigarettes, her lighter, and her last ten dollars—her train money [home to Dorchester]. She was bawling, and I was telling her, 'Just try to relax.' I didn't want to start crying. I had to go in this tank with all these guys. And the first sign they think you're a punk [prison jargon for a victim of sexual assault], they're going to try to do something to you," he told Holly Millea in the May 1998 issue of *Premiere* magazine. "So I'm trying to hold my shit in, and they're shackling me up, and my mom's crying and trying to hold on to me, and the guards are pulling me away."

Being imprisoned with seasoned criminals was the downside. The upside was that Plymouth housed several of Mark's friends from Dorchester. "I felt like everybody in my neighborhood was in the same house of corrections, and my brother was doing time, so I figured there was nothing to worry about."

His older brother Jim was doing ten years for armed robbery. Drugs, according to Mark, had also led Jim to the same place. "He got high, went crazy, tried to rob the train station," Mark said. Remarkably, by the time Mark landed at Plymouth his brother had become a role model for sobriety. "Jimbo cleaned up his act. He was running the drug program in prison."

Mark's short stay of only forty-five days at Plymouth was a transformational experience, a pivotal turning point where the teen thug could have easily turned into a career criminal. In prison Mark realized that he wanted "more out of life," he said years later, after he had indeed gotten quite a bit more out of the world.

During his time at Plymouth, Wahlberg was touched by an angel. A prison volunteer, whom Wahlberg will only identify by the pseudonym Emily, singled out the cherubic-faced con for redemption.

He told Jan Stuart in the November 1, 1997, edition of the *Los Angeles Times*, "I call Emily my aunt now. She goes to prison, to churches, to elderly homes and prays with people. I was the youngest person ever in that facility. She saw me and went [in a thick Irish brogue], 'God, you're just a baby. Oh, darlin', what are you doing here?' She would come and pray with me and pray for me. Once I realized I had taken the wrong route, then all my faith came back in a much more profound way than before.

"When I left there I never thought I would see her again. And fate brought us back together. I was out in California, my record was about to come out [in 1991], my brother . . . asked this guy from Massachusetts who was living in California to kind of watch out for me and keep me out of trouble. We were hanging out, and he asked me to take him home. We walked into the house, and Emily walked by, this angel who had changed my life. I said, 'Who's that?' And he said, 'My mother.' I said, 'I know your mother.' And she came back in and ran up to me and kissed and hugged me. It was so wild," a tearful Wahlberg recalled in the November 1, 1997, issue of the *Los Angeles Times*.

While Emily served as a positive role model for Mark in prison, perhaps even more effective were the negative role models there. All Wahlberg had to do was look around the exercise yard to see the "ghosts of his Christmas futures." Friends only a few years older were doing ten to twenty-five years at Plymouth. Their aging faces, Mark said, scared him straight.

While transformational, his time at Plymouth was also emotional hell. Just before going to prison, he fell in love for the first time. When the girl's father found out about Mark's new address, Plymouth Rock, he forced her to break off the relationship.

Mark was devastated. "She didn't even wait for me. Only fifty-something days and she didn't wait for me! My dreams were shattered. Crushed me. It's still there. Believe me. I can almost laugh about it now, because I can't cry about it anymore," he said in his interview with Holly Millea in the May 1998 issue of *Premiere* magazine.

Prison not only transformed Wahlberg spiritually, it also turned him into one hot stud. Again, there was a choice to be made, a fork in the road, with one path leading to drug addiction and no doubt a lifetime of recidivism. Instead, Wahlberg picked the other path, pumping iron, which would eventually lead to a ten-story-high billboard in Times Square and the cover of *Rolling Stone*.

"I got locked up, and I didn't have nothing else to do. I could either go out into the yard and get high with these guys and drink home brew and shake people down, or I could stay in and work out and not get into trouble. Make it as quick a process as possible and get the hell out of there," he said.

Plymouth was "not something I'm proud of, but it changed my life, you know? One of the worst things that ever happened to me made me the person I am today. You might want to take your brain out of your head and wash it and scrub it and make it clean, but you can't. You've got to learn from your experiences," he told *Interview* magazine in October 1997.

The slammer wasn't all sculpted bodies and visits from Emily. There's at least one image Wahlberg would like to "scrub" out of his memory, but nine years after the fact he could still describe the scene in X-rated detail. And it's not a pretty picture.

In a remarkably candid interview with *Rolling Stone*, Mark recalled, "This was when I first got in, on the first tier, new man's section on the flat. I woke up. This dude was sticking his private area through the bars, letting some other dude lick on it. I was like, 'What the fuck?!' I mean, boy!"

After forty-five days of spiritual and physical reconstruction, Wahlberg had a new bod and mind-set, but his prospects didn't look good. He was a ninth-grade dropout with a prison record and no job skills.

Although his mother once had called him lackadaisical, after his release from Plymouth, Mark seems to have turned into an overachiever in overalls. His first job after prison was driving a tow truck. Then he did construction and worked as an orderly in a hospital. And as much as he hated formal education, Wahlberg took courses to become an auto mechanic.

Mark came from blue collar, and he was never ashamed of his roots. In fact, he embraced them and recalled with pride his stint as a bricklayer's apprentice: "I was happy with that job, because it was something that made me feel good. To build a wall for the side of a building really felt good to me. It was an accomplishment. One building we rebuilt was a place I used to hang out at, and it was weird to see my name all over its walls!"

Despite these potentially dead-end jobs, Mark remained optimistic because he had connections. While brother Jimbo had been a pen pal, another sibling had become a major recording star as a member of the New Kids on the Block.

CHAPTER 4

Billion-Dollar Bubblegum

Packaged and sweetened in the recording studio by Maurice Starr, the Svengali of benzoyl peroxide bubblegum, New Kids on the Block became a music-industry phenomenon in the late 1980s and early 1990s, releasing multiplatinum albums of techno-Muzak. The group consisted of the four friends from the bus Donnie had recommended to Starr: Jordan Knight, Jordan's brother Jonathan, Danny Wood, plus the group's heartthrob, whom Starr had unearthed on his own, Joe McIntyre.

Although the screaming girls in the audience thought all the New Kids were studs, McIntyre's movie-star good looks made him a standout in a group of outstanding-looking young guys.

After the New Kids began touring, Donnie was rarely home. The two youngest Wahlbergs had never been separated, and Mark felt his older brother's absence keenly.

"When I was growing up, Donnie was sort of a cross between a big brother and a hero to me. We were best buddies and used to hang out together all the time. When he started to spend all of his time at rehearsals, we drifted apart . . . and suddenly . . . he was famous. I hardly saw him at all for ages. We really grew apart," Mark said in *Marky Mark and the Funky Bunch*.

Donnie was not only famous, he was rich. Never a tall-tale teller, Mark said that over the years his hero earned $115 million as a New Kid. The New Kids' debut album, *Hangin' Tough*, went quadruple platinum when it was released in 1989. A year later, the New Kids' 900-number logged 125,000 calls a day at fifty cents a pop. You do the math.

Their concerts and extensive merchandising (New Kids lunch boxes, action figures, New Kids bedspreads with the Kids spread-eagled on them), brought in almost $1 billion a year! That's a lot of weekly allowances from teenaged girls around the world. In 1991, *Fortune* magazine proclaimed the group the top money-making entertainers in the world, outgrossing rock superstars like Rod Stewart and even movie stars like Arnold Schwarzenegger (despite his take from the number one movie hit of 1991, *Terminator 2: Judgment Day).*

Nevertheless, fame and wealth didn't distract Donnie from looking out for his younger brother. He felt the same sense of loss and separation as Mark did. So Donny came up with a simple but generous solution to this separation anxiety. He invited Mark to go on the road with the band.

Touring was an alternate universe for a kid who had been humiliated by using food stamps, jammed in a bedroom with five siblings, and later sentenced to prison. Instead of government-subsidized food, Mark stayed in luxury hotel suites and got to ring room service for cheeseburgers at two in the morning.

Donnie encouraged tiny extravagances like burgers on demand since the Kids were doing McDonald's-size business. The New Kids lived a fantasy life which they shared with their entourage, including Mark. Perks for the kids included limousines, deluxe tour buses, the most expensive Nintendo games du jour, bodyguards that scared even a tough ex-con like Mark, plus all those adoring groupies willing to provide in one observer's euphemism, "female companionship" to any New Kid or, lucky Marky, a New Kid's kid brother.

Groupies didn't confine themselves to New Kids' concerts. Teenage girls camped out in front of the Wahlbergs' Dorchester triplex, trampling the tiny front lawn for a peek inside. However, they wanted to see Donnie, not Mark.

Eventually, the groupies turned into voyeurs. Mom Alma recalled these pubescent Peeping Toms: "We were in bed one evening, and fans were peeking in our living-room window. . . . They were playing New Kids music out in front of the house at 2:00 A.M. and calling for Donnie to come out! We've had our phone number changed three times."

Alma decided to organize this devoted mob and became president of the New Kids' official fan club. She also found a new fan for herself. After eight exhausting years as a single mom, Alma fell in love and married Mark Conroy in 1990.

Despite his problems with authority and discipline in the past, Mark immediately bonded with his new stepdad. Conroy was anything but a wicked stepfather. Just as Mark began to feel the loss of Donnie to the glamorous life on the road, Conroy volunteered to be his new best buddy. His stepfather never tried to replace Donald Senior as head of the family or as disciplinarian. Instead, he and Mark became as inseparable as Donnie and Mark had once been.

The two Marks coexisted as equals. It was a wise parenting move on Conroy's part. Mark had never accepted discipline at home or school, and a stern stepdad would have been intolerable to him.

Donnie's wedding present to the new bride and groom was a sprawling home in the upscale Boston suburb of Braintree, Massachusetts. The modern-style structure boasted a swimming pool and Jacuzzi. Also, in the backyard, there was a regulation-height basketball hoop for the six Wahlberg boys.

To keep teenage girls suffering estrogen rage from looking in the windows as they had at the Dorchester apartment, Donnie reluctantly erected a six-foot-high fence around the house in Braintree. The fence came in handy after a local newspaper printed the family's new address, and fans renewed their assault on the Wahlberg camp.

To this day Mark divides his time between Los Angeles and the family home in Braintree, ten miles south of Boston. At his parents' residence, he occupies a home within a home that gives him privacy while still maintaining contact with the rest of the family down the hall. Actually, his "home" is a single room, "like a little apartment. Kinda small, really," he said. The apartment sounds more like a bachelor pad, crammed with goodies that the poor boy from Dorchester once could only dream about: a fireplace, kitchenette, and a souped-up stereo system.

When Mark wants to watch big-screen TV, however, he goes to the main family area, which has a giant television set, eight feet by eight feet, whose screen automatically descends from the ceiling. Mark's favorite programming is professional boxing.

The Wahlberg family home wasn't the only recipient of Donnie's lavish generosity. In 1990, the same year Donnie bought the family a home, he bought Mark wheels: a black Jeep Cherokee. Mark loved the gift. "It's my favorite place to be in the whole world," he enthused. Later, after his own money started to pour in, Mark souped up the car with $10,000 worth of stereo equipment. "It's the most unbelievable sound system you ever heard. . . . I have eighteen ten-inch subwoofers, five amplifiers, one thousand watts of power. Shit-hot!"

When Mark wasn't tooling around in every youth's dream vehicle, he could often be found at a less-than-glamorous spot, the Dorchester Youth Collaborative. There, in 1990, he began to study seriously for the high-school diploma equivalency test, the GED.

The collaborative is a drop-in and hang-out center where kids who have done time are referred post-release. Mark made the place his second home.

"It's a youth center where kids like me hang out to get away from trouble. It's a great place that helps lots of kids. They just tell you, 'You screwed up. Look at your life.'"

CHAPTER 5

A Rap Star Is Born

Mark looked at his life in 1990, saw a precipice in front of himself, and stepped back from it. Then he stepped up—to a career that would eventually surpass his "hero" Donnie's gilded life of five-star hotels and take-your-pick girlfriends.

So what does a wannabe singing star with no vocal talent but lots of charisma and a body by Fischer do? He becomes a rap singer.

Donnie didn't take his brother's rejection of the band and its "ballady" style personally. Creatively, Donnie turned out to be as good a Svengali to Mark as Maurice Starr had been to him. Perhaps even better, since Donnie let Mark flourish in a medium he loved, rap, rather than the pop arena which Starr had so lucratively penned the New Kids into.

Mark knew a few basic dance steps, and he could do the rapper's classic "strut" perfectly. Donnie composed some rap songs (if "song" is the right term for talking instead of singing).

Only two years Mark's senior, Donnie *was* and *is* the kind of older brother everyone would love to have. On the road with the New Kids, instead of being career-obsessed and self-obsessed, the senior Wahlberg was brooding about the baby of the family, who after prison clearly needed fraternal guidance. Donnie supplied it magnificently.

Donnie recalls, "I was writing songs for all these other people just for fun. I said, 'Mark, I'm going to do one for you.'" Then as many young people with typical MTV short attention spans do, Donnie promptly forgot about his promise.

His baby brother, however, didn't forget the promise, and reminded him until Donnie made good on it. Donnie said, "Every time I called home, Mark would say, 'Where's that song you were gonna do for me?' That's when I realized he was serious. So I got serious about it too."

Donnie was generous with his time, but a martinet with Marky. After an all-night marathon session of rap-writing at home in Braintree, Donnie would roust Mark from bed and make him practice what they had composed the night before. Mark eventually surpassed his brother's talent as a lyricist, and years later his compositions ended up on movie soundtracks.

Time wasn't the only thing Donnie was generous with. With his wealth from the New Kids' royalties, he paid cash to self-produce his brother's demo tape. In 1991, when the sample cut was circulated to all the record labels, New Kid Donnie was hot, and anything or anyone associated with him shared the heat. Interscope Records, a label owned by the conglomerate Warner/Elektra/Atlantic, wanted to be in the Donnie Wahlberg business so it took on his brother as a way to grease the relationship with Donnie.

Donnie had other motivations besides brotherly love. He loved to write, and Starr hadn't let him contribute a single cut to the New Kids' early albums, including their self-titled debut album (1987) and *Hangin' Tough* (1989). The boys had grown up on rap, and Donnie was stuck doing Barry Manilow lite, Muzak with lyrics. Rejecting Starr's smothering influence, he remembered the New Kids' co-creator, Mary Alford, and asked her to manage Mark and co-produce his debut album.

Long before rap became a multibillion-dollar business, it was discovered by inner-city children of all colors. Mark remembered hearing his first rap song at age four. He claims he immediately sat down and composed a reverential imitation, unlikely for a preliterate preschooler, but a nice memory to add to the Marky Mark mythology.

On all those formative bus rides to Mrs. Trotter's, where Mark and his classmates did impromptu rap sets, the future New Kids on the bus didn't sing Karen Carpenter or a medley of Debbie Boone's greatest hit. Their influences were rap groups now lost to memory, Grandmaster Flash, Afrika Bambaattaa, and what one history of the Funky Bunch with no sense of irony referred to as "the *more obscure* Molly Moll."

Off the bus, Mark took to the streets—Dorchester, Roxbury, and Mattapan—with only a boombox as his backup band. There he perfected his breakdance and lyrical improvisations with friends like Rasta Phil and Brizia, who later became his bodyguards.

"Sometimes I'd rhyme about this, sometimes I'd rhyme about that. Sometimes I'd get stuck, then other times, I'd be hanging around in a daze, and then all of a sudden, I'd come up with rap. Half the time I didn't have a pen to write it down," he said in *Marky Mark and the Funky Bunch* (1992).

Soon, Mark took his act indoors. First to parties, then to Boston-area clubs. Two months after taping a demo, a polished album (*Music for the People*) hit the music stores on July 23, 1991, from Atlantic Records' Interscope label.

The album surprised Donnie's fans from his New Kids incarnation, but as producer, Donnie must have felt liberated by the freedom of writing raw rap instead of the New Kids' syrupy lyrics.

The New Kids crooned about teen love; Donnie and Mark rapped about racial hatred and substance abuse. It's hard to determine who took more pride in the project, Donnie or Mark. Donnie's artistic influence infused the CD.

Produced by Donnie D. Productions, Donnie did all the arrangements, most of the writing, the backup vocals, and even performed a few solos on the album. Donnie forgave Starr for having rejected his own songs when he was a member of the New Kids on the Block and accepted several raps penned by Starr. If they listened closely, New Kids fans could hear Jordan Knight singing backup on one track. If they checked the credits, another Kid, Danny Wood, wrote and produced one song. Mary Alford earned her manager's fee by hiring MC Spice, a well-known Boston rap artist, and deejay Terry Yancey, for the recording.

Music for the People sounded different from most previous rap records. Its most startling innovation was the use of live guitar and bass. Prior to this, rap records had generally used prerecorded drums and bass. The guitars took some of the edge off the nails-on-chalkboard effect many people experience when listening to rap, especially the scratchy noise created by the deejay's fingertips on vinyl.

As a standard promotional tool, the album needed multiple videos for MTV, so five dancers and a deejay dubbed the Funky Bunch were added to enhance the visuals. The new troupe then hit the road to promote their product.

"We just wanted to do an album together—just us," Donnie said. *Music for the People* entered the charts at number 39 and stayed there for a marathon forty weeks! The album went almost triple platinum, selling 1.4 million CDs and cassettes.

Four singles also sold well. "Good Vibrations," the first solo off the album, debuted at number eleven on *Billboard*'s "Hot 100" list in July, made it all the way to number 2, and sold 770,000 copies. "Wildside" followed in October, with 637,000 discs, then the by-now ironically titled "I Need Money," which sold 72,000 copies after its February 1992 release. Finally, "Peace," in May, performed calmly with sales of 43,000.

The video of *Music for the People,* released in 1992, sold 16,000 copies, an impressive showing for a format that sells far less than recorded music, according to the music-tracking service, SoundScan, which provided these sales figures.

"Good Vibrations," unlike so many other rap songs, offered a healthy message of "Just say no." In 1991, it was a perfect vector into the white community horrified by rap's excesses. Mark joked about the first single, "It's a track that could make George Bush move!" The lyrics of "Wildside" condemned substance abuse, racism, and gang violence. They were also autobiographical, as Mark suggested when he said, "The story I'm tellin' is all about things that happened in and around Boston, very serious things that I thought were important for me to speak about, like racial tension in the Boston area. It's a very serious issue." Mark had personally experienced this "issue," paid the price, and shared the life-changing lessons he had learned.

Music for the People took on a lot of controversial issues swirling around rap. One was euphemistically referred to as "sampling"—inserting music into a rap song from a non-rap artist's record without paying royalties. Not surprisingly, the original artists had different names for sampling—like *plagiarism* and *copyright infringement*! Unlike other rap artists, Mark acknowledged widespread "sampling" on his album by crediting the sampled artist in the liner notes—and paying fat royalties.

The biggest issue, which he also confronted without worrying about being politically correct, tackled the debate about white rap. Was the genre a black art form which white record producers had appropriated for white kids? Mark vehemently denied the charge and insisted color was irrelevant as long as the artist remained "true to the art form."

Already super-rich, Donnie valued his brother's success in non-economic terms. "Any Top Ten success is just icing on the cake," he said. Mark felt the same. "This record has brought us back together." A picture in *People* magazine around the time *Music for the People* debuted, shows Donnie with his hands all over Mark's face, squeezing his cheeks with one hand, pushing down on his head with the other. Mark grimaces in mock pain.

The Wahlberg boys needed each other's emotional support when the reviews came out. To call them mixed understates the dramatic range of adulation and condemnation from the press.

Entertainment Weekly gave Mark high marks for his gritty style and content, describing the rapper-songwriter as "admirably willing to grapple with urban themes." The magazine also placed him in the vanguard of rap trendsetters: "He has the goods to lead rap music into its next artistic phase."

Interview magazine, more hip to hip-hop, was positively lyrical about the Bunch's funky lyrics and style, calling their debut album "a slugfest of contagious hip-hop and synthesized funk from the spiritual calisthenics of 'Good Vibrations,' to the down-and-dirty 'Bout Time I Funk You.'" The white-bread *New York Daily News* said anemically, "The music is fun. It's enjoyable street music."

Not everyone, however, was pleased. The authoritative *Rolling Stone*, which would one day put Mark Wahlberg on its cover, found another place to put him at this time. The magazine dumped him in the Worst Male Singer category, embarrassingly shared with Michael Bolton, Axl Rose, Prince, and Vanilla Ice, whom *Rolling Stone* suggested sample Procul Harum's "A Whiter Shade of Pale" on *his* next album.

Music for the People's sales showed that buyers liked what they heard. The second single, "Wildside," spent twenty weeks on the pop charts and ten weeks on the rap charts. Record buyers liked the music, but what they liked even more was Mark, the "hunkasaurus," as *Entertainment Weekly* described him. The video version of "Good Vibrations" was financed by Mark and

Donnie, instead of the label, to ensure artistic control. It became the most-requested video on MTV during the summer of 1991.

And while the professionals either carped or raved, the public not only voted with its dollars, it filled out survey forms in magazines and voted the Funky Bunch into one awards show after another on both sides of the Atlantic. *Rolling Stone* might call him a "pale imitation" of Vanilla Ice and question his gangsta credentials, but the Boston Music Awards voted Mark plus his Bunch the Best New *Rap* Act (emphasis added). Magazine readers felt the boys couldn't make a false move. The United Kingdom's *Smash Hits* magazine poll voted the group Best *Dance* Act (emphasis added)! All that prancing down the aisles of the school bus en route to Mrs. Trotter's elementary had finally paid off.

Mark, once tow-truck-bound jobwise, flew to England to accept his smashing choreography award. In an acceptance speech, Mark made sure to thank the people who conducted the poll, the writers and publisher of *Smash Hits*. "I can't believe it! I've won! This is the best award I could've won, the best category, too. I knew about the *Smash Hits* awards. I knew they was [sic] important because Donnie has always told me that *Smash Hits* is the 'mag daddy,' but I never really thought I'd get one this soon. Being a new group, you never know what people are gonna think, but now I'm really excited. I'm real glad we've taken off. This award is proof, man."

Mark's high praise for a magazine unknown on his side of the Atlantic underlined his conscientious care and feeding of the press. The critics might question his red-blood-cell count, but he knew the press could make or break an artist in the public eye, make him a hip dude or a figure of fun.

A picture from 1991 shows Mark at his most press-friendly. He has his arm around an ancient-looking woman, the self-described "world's oldest rock critic," seventy-something Jane Scott of the *Cleveland Plain Dealer*. Hey, man! They buy CDs in

Cleveland, too, and a positive review from Scott would make them want to buy more. At nineteen, Mark was already displaying the brilliant career self-management that would transform him from the butt of jokes in *Rolling Stone* into its cover subject (twice) and ultimately, into a major movie star!

If there's an IQ test for street smarts, Mark would score at genius level. In other areas, like finances, the youngster showed he was no accountant. At nineteen, only three years out of Plymouth and the cab of a tow truck, Mark Wahlberg had become very rich and fairly famous. What he did with these two slings and arrows of outrageous good fortune would make him even more famous, but less rich.

Broke, in fact.

CHAPTER 6

Show and Sell

Publicity stunts are a tricky business. Almost any miscreant can manipulate the media for fifteen minutes of infamy. Slap a cop, go to jail, appear on TV's *Hard Copy*. Go to McDonald's with a multiple murderer, land a recording contract, guest-host a few talk shows, then disappear into your place of origin, the woodwork.

The Zsa Zsa Gabors and Kato Kaelins of this world have figured out how to get even the crème de la crème of celebrity journalists like Barbara Walters and Diane Sawyer to chat them up for a while before the public goes on to its next source of morbid fascination. A true genius of media manipulation, however, keeps the spotlight on himself long enough to launch a career and then keep it airborne. When it came to media smarts, Mark was the Einstein of promotional savvy. His debut album's platinum sales made him white-hot, but most recording stars supernova and then expire.

Quick, name Vanilla Ice's first album, which went quadruple platinum. At this point, you're more likely asking yourself, "Vanilla who?" The careers of pop/rap stars with modest talent but a great publicity machine behind them typically have the shelf life of dairy products. On the cover of *Rolling Stone* today, selling abdominal-crunch equipment on TV infomercials tomorrow.

Perhaps one of the most street-smart guys to come from the streets, Wahlberg knew that if he didn't want to be yesterday's news, like Menudo, he would have to separate himself from the pack of superannuated teen idols.

Simply, elegantly, and cannily, Mark decided to expose himself in public. We're not talking full disclosure, as in the final scene of *Boogie Nights*, but PG-13 enough to shock parents and enthrall teenage girls on estrogen overload. The *New York Times* recognized his savvy: Tease the kids, but don't traumatize their parents who pay for the records and concert tickets. Or, as the *Times* phrased it, "His live shows turned into stripteases that coyly stopped short of full exposure."

The first unveiling of Marky Mark took place on a sweltering day in July 1991 at Magic Mountain, an amusement park thirty minutes north of Los Angeles. (The park has been called Disneyland with scarier rides, but Magic Mountain attracts the same family crowd as the Magic Kingdom.) *Rolling Stone* said the rap artist didn't become a "true phenomenon until after a performance" at the famous park. Already topless, instead of performing one more song—the usual way to do an encore—Wahlberg dropped his pants.

Never great at impulse control, as his prison sentence suggested, Wahlberg claimed he did it as a lark without premeditation. However, the reaction convinced him to make the moment a permanent part of his stage act. "I had never seen so many camera flashes and such a crazy reaction," he said of his first time. "When you're onstage, you're the center of attention. You have to do that—not pull down your pants, but do whatever it is to keep interest. I was kind of coming into my own, finding out what people liked and what they didn't. . . . It was just one of those things, man. I was doing something kinda berserk and I just dropped my pants.

I saw fifty million flashes, and I was like, 'Oh, shit!' I was like, 'This might be something.' Then it started getting a little out of hand."

To his horror, Mark found himself compelled by concert-goers to continue what had begun as a lark and turned into an albatross around his ankles. "My fans tend to demand it," he said two years later.

His brother Donnie didn't think the impromptu striptease was impromptu or impulsive at all. It was a calculated move to hold on to a crowd whose attention was divided between the Funky Bunch and a Latino rap group, which was also performing that day at the park.

Donnie recalled (in 1992's *Marky Mark* by Marky Mark and Lynn Goldsmith), "The crowd was about fifty percent girls and fifty percent Mexican kids who came to see the other rap group on the bill. They were starting to compete with the girls who were there to see Marky. We were trying to think of what he could do to get the guys on his side. When he came out, he dropped his pants. It was hilarious. I couldn't stop laughing. He started dancing around the stage. . . . It was funny to see my little brother onstage in his drawers. I didn't think he should keep doing it, but it was so funny that I couldn't tell him to stop. I kept wanting to see him do it again!"

From Donnie's cryptic comment, it's hard to figure out how flashing his underwear would "get the guys on his side," unless, of course, he was referring to the other important demographic that worships Mark and all his merchandise. Besides pubescent girls, adult gays loved the new Mark in briefs. A brilliant self-marketer, Wahlberg knew that gay men often set trends and create stars. Donna Summer hung out in gay discos and was discovered in that milieu. More famously, Bette Midler launched her career performing at a gay sex club, the Continental Baths, in New York City.

While Wahlberg wasn't about to strap a towel around his middle and sashay down the corridors of a bathhouse singing show tunes to turbocharge his career, he was willing to pop up at gay bars for the same reason. In the quaint phrasing of the decorous *New York Times*, Wahlberg's apparitions at gay discos accomplished this: "The entertainment mogul David Geffen became *aware* of him and whispered a piece of advice in the ear of his friend Calvin Klein."

Geffen came out of the closet a few years ago at an AIDS fund-raiser in Los Angeles, beginning his speech, "As a gay man, I . . ." Klein has been dragged out of the closet kicking and screaming in at least one biography he failed to suppress. Both magnates are notoriously tight-lipped, so we'll never know exactly what Geffen said to Klein, but it may have gone something like this: "Have you seen the abs on this kid!? Why don't you hire him to sell your underwear?"

A male reporter for the *New York Times* described Mark's anatomy as "torpedo-sized biceps, pecs like wrought-iron balconies and an abdomen he can ripple at will." Jon Pareles wrote that in the *Times*' "At Lunch With . . ." column, a format the newspaper usually reserved for the likes of Salman Rushdie and Philip Roth.

Mark's record label, Atlantic/Interscope, saw a commercial tie-in and contacted record producer Jimmy Iovine, who was a personal friend of Geffen's. Geffen made the introduction to Klein. Mark described the networking: "You know, David and Calvin are cool with each other. So they called me up, and it was like, 'Yo, Calvin wants to hook up with you—he wants to meet you and stuff.' I was like, 'Really?' You know, he's just been so la-a-rge. I mean, even in [Boston's blue-collar] neighborhoods, if you had a pair of Calvin Kleins, you was the man. So I went to his house and I met him, hooked up," he told George Wayne in the January 1993 issue of *Vanity Fair*.

Klein invited Mark over, and when he showed up, David Geffen was already there. "Geffen was just hanging out. We were just talking," Wahlberg said.

Both men told him they wanted Mark to be their label bearer. "The only reason we want you is because you were doing your own thing, and that's what we want you to do for us. We think it's cool," Wahlberg said, recalling his conversation with Klein and Geffen.

"Calvin said he would like Herb Ritts to shoot me," Mark also has remembered. Ritts is a top photographer and arguably the best at exposing the male physique at its most spectacular and erotic. Even at this early stage in his career, Wahlberg knew Ritts' pedigree and agreed at once, without discussing payment. "Well, you can get me to do the pictures if Herb is going to take them! 'Cause Herb Ritts is the man!" he told Klein.

Before you could say "spokesmodel," Klein had signed the twenty-one-year-old rapper to a contract and put his torso on the map—as well as on billboards across the country and page after page of *GQ* ads. Mark made the cover of *Esquire* (tied to a tree, screaming in pain like an Annie Leibowitz rendering of Edvard Munch). A serious analysis of his body parts in the January 1993 issue of *Vanity Fair* managed to be both semiotic and idiotic at the same time, with the interviewer, George Wayne, making this request, which Mark granted: "Can you take off your shirt, get on your hands, and give me fifty push-ups?"

The number one celeb magazine also hailed him as "the number one poster boy for every gay man in America," and *Genre* magazine mentioned all the posters "yellowing on the walls of many a gay man's bedroom."

While Wahlberg got a huge career boost from the underwear campaign, Klein did even better. Mark only earned a hundred grand for his grandstanding, but the jockey maker enjoyed a jump in sales of thirty-seven percent, surpassing the record previously set by Brooke Shields' "kiddie porn" commercials of a decade earlier.

David Geffen described the impression Wahlberg's giant image created; "It made him iconic. He was perfect for what we were looking for."

The young man didn't complain about the fee. And he was grateful for the free samples that came with the deal. "After a while I was sick of paying $18 for underwear," he said.

About this time, an even more striking photo of Wahlberg appeared in *People* magazine. In the picture there's Mark, shirtless, beyond buffed as always, but his overalls are being pulled *up*, not *down*, by his mother. Alma Wahlberg and her son both sport big smiles in the photo.

In a photo in his 1992 autobiography, Mrs. Wahlberg is again yanking up her son's pants, but this time she seems to be grimacing rather than grinning. Alma wasn't crazy about her son acting like a male stripper. At first, she tried subtle hints, like leaving belts and suspenders around the house. When that didn't work, she consoled herself with the fact that there were several layers of protection between Mark and gaping, groping fans.

"When I first heard he dropped his pants, I asked, 'Why do you have to do that?' I offered him suspenders and belts and whatever it would take to hold them up. But I knew that even when he did it, he had running shorts on *underneath*, so it wasn't too, too upsetting to me," Alma said in *Marky Mark* (1992) by Marky Mark and Lynn Goldsmith.

However, on another occasion, when Donnie pulled Mark's underwear down at a concert, he didn't have on running shorts or anything else.

A bit of information Wahlberg told another magazine is equally telling, and in this case, words are worth a thousand pictures. "Somebody was nice enough to give me a couple of those original pictures, the famous ones of me in my underwear. My mother's keeping 'em for a while," he told Mark Marrel in the October 1994 issue of *Interview* magazine.

Although Mrs. Wahlberg wasn't crazy about her son running around the house with his pants falling down, she enjoyed the sight when it was frozen in time, especially at her hometown department store. "That was artwork as far as I was concerned," his mother said about the underwear shots. "It was so exciting. I'd go into [downtown Boston's] Filene's, and he'd be hanging from the ceiling."

Wahlberg soon grew to hate the marketing campaign that had turned him into a skyscraper-size slab of beef. He carped that he felt like a "statue" in Times Square. Statues don't sing or rap, and the flesh-peddling had been done to promote his music, not his muscles. "People were really looking for the exploitation of Marky Mark," he said bitterly, and the Calvin Klein campaign was his photo-op pimp.

Some days, it seemed, he wished he had never dropped his drawers. "The underwear thing is semi-haunting me. That's not what I want to be remembered for. People loved it—wow, this kid's running around on TV in his underwear. Now that I got them interested, though, I want to make a good impression."

Wahlberg's unofficial biographer, Randi Reisfeld, in her otherwise adulatory 1992 book, *Marky Mark and the Funky Bunch*, suggested Mark enjoyed showing it off, rather than feeling exploited by demanding fans and Madison Avenue. "Marky clearly gets off on the crowd reaction—the louder they cheer, the lower his pants go," Reisfeld wrote. Reisfeld, a former editor at *16 Magazine*, also claimed that Mark walked around backstage in his underwear. Females, the author noted, are not allowed backstage.

Mrs. Wahlberg claimed her son's exhibitionism began *long* before he decided it was merely a good career move. By the time he was three, Alma said, other family members noticed Mark had fallen in love with his reflection in anything shiny. "It could be the toaster or the oven and he would climb up on top of the counter and sit in front of it and, you know, trying to flex his muscles when all there was was little bones!" Eventually, 40,000 fans per show and innumerable videos would replace his first "stage," the funhouse mirror of a toaster!

Donnie Wahlberg joined Klein in exposing his sibling's best assets. If PG-rated frontal nudity could make his brother a national figure, imagine what an R-rated view from behind could accomplish! At the end of a spring 1992 pay-per-view concert, the first ever with a "Parental Discretion Advised" label, Donnie grabbed his brother by the shoulders and turned him away from the audience. Then instead of just pulling down Mark's pants, Donnie pulled down his Calvins as well.

A reporter from the *New York Times* covered the uncovering: "Onstage, Marky Mark stripped to his underwear: thigh-length black Calvin Kleins. He turned his back to the crowd, and Donnie Wahlberg, who joined his brother for the finale, pulled the drawers down to reveal black briefs."

Why was Mark wearing two pairs of underwear? the reporter failed to ask. Was it for protection, an extra layer of defense, from just this kind of smash-and-grab harassment, usually performed by female fans, not a brother/mentor? The journalist didn't say, but continued, "As the girls up front squealed and clasped one another, [Donnie] pulled those halfway off to reveal Marky Mark's bare skin. It was only a moment, only a glimpse. For a rapper seeking respect, anything more might be flaunting it."

A unique illustration of brotherly love and career management combined, a picture from the pay-per-view concert published in *Movie Buff Newsletter* shows Donnie with his left hand tugging at Mark's underwear to reveal a butt for which the term "bubble" was coined.

The *New York Times* might call it flaunting, but Mark called it exploitation. At times, sexual harassment seemed a more accurate term. At a gala movie premiere, Brooke Shields, in a magnificent Donna Karan gown, playfully accosted Mark—in something less couture-ish (T-shirt and ripped jeans)—and pulled down his pants, revealing that his abs were even more ripped than his jeans.

The incident, immortalized in *People*, shows two things. Wahlberg was still doing free product placement for Calvin Klein, because you can see the logo on his jockeys even in the blurry shot. Even more visible in the photo is his embarrassment. While it might be the dream of every teenage boy to get "pantsed" by Brooke Shields, the expression on Wahlberg's face looks anything but dreamy. If a guy did that to a girl at such a public event, it might be called sexual assault. A lawsuit, maybe an arrest, would be made, rather than a tongue-in-cheek (pun intended) caption with pic in a national magazine.

Sometimes Mark got tired of being treated like a piece of meat by women who thought they were being cute rather than annoying. In 1992, when Amanda de Cadenet, a London talk-show host, grabbed two meaty handfuls of her guest's chest, he returned the gesture and copped a feel. The moment has been immortalized on videotape.

Mark defended his behavior with im*pec*cable logic: "She felt *my* breasts. She's got nice big breasts. I'd love to feel them. I'd love to suck them. There's nothing wrong with that, shit! She's a woman, I'm a man. She has big titties and I'd love to suck them if I had the chance. I'd love to do lots of things to her—what's wrong with that? That's not bad. What's so dirty about feeling someone's breasts? It's like, you don't think girls *want* me to feel their breasts? People made a big deal out of me grabbing her breasts—why? She said to me, 'I heard you have a very big chest.' And I said, 'I heard *you* have a very big chest too. And as a matter of fact, I think yours is a little bigger than mine.' And she said, 'Why don't we find out?' And I said, 'Great, I'm glad you asked me, because I was gonna ask you,'" he noted in *Marky Mark and the Funky Bunch*.

Mark added later that he felt a bit embarrassed about the conversation since the talk-show host was pregnant. "But she wanted to measure my chest." Besides, Mark wasn't the one who had brought up the subject of comparative anatomy. "Victim," however, was not the term being applied to Mark, no matter how much he felt like one after being grabbed by a pregnant talk-show hostess.

Soon Mark developed a strict "hands-off" policy when it came to female fans who got touchy-feely, as he said in his 1992 biography: "I've met a lot of twenty-five- and thirty-year-old women who have seen me on MTV. They want to rub my chest and all this nonsense. I always say to them, 'You want me to take off my shirt?' How would I sound coming up to you and saying, 'Take off *your* shirt'? They're trying to exploit me to the fullest."

When and if Mark took off his shirt and dropped his jeans, it would be to sell product, not himself. "I'll still work out, and in my shows I'll still take off my shirt and stuff. Then again, I'm not going to go out there and just flaunt it." Unless it was to sell albums or concert tickets.

The backlash against the sexy show-off began almost immediately. Wahlberg could have made the male equivalent of Kelly LeBrock's plea in the famous TV shampoo commercial: "Don't hate me because I'm buffed!" However, people did, and "hate" might be too mild a term. The only thing the public likes to do more than build up its heroes is tear them down, an expert on the subject, Prince Charles, once told Barbara Walters.

The billboards on the Sunset Strip in West Hollywood were too sturdy to tear down, however, so Marky bashers settled for defacing them with excrement. "People used to throw shit at my billboard. I'd drive by and see paint stains and shit," Wahlberg said.

Fame as a rap star and billboard demigod didn't go to his head, but the ensuing wealth made him dizzy and improvident. Especially after his handlers renegotiated his contract with Calvin Klein, when the jump in Klein's sales figures was reported in the *Wall Street Journal* and *Tiger Beat*. Like many poor people, most famously Lotto winners who get rich quick, Wahlberg didn't know how to hold on to his money. The first royalty check from his debut album was cashed and blown immediately, leaving him the New Broke Kid on the Block in Braintree.

"Like my first big check I ever got, I went and spent the whole thing—$100,000—on one thing. I bought a car. I didn't have the money for gas. See, I kind of learned the hard way. I was the only guy where I grew up that had a Mercedes. That was stupid because everybody was trying to steal it, or smash it, or crash it, or something. I would literally cancel a show just so I could go home and drive my car."

His nouveau poverty didn't last long. The first fat royalty check was just a harbinger of future riches as his debut album and singles made the initial $100,000 seem like lunch money.

Mark was soon sticking up ATM machines with his cash card—in a reverse case of earlier muggings—and handing over huge amounts of currency to delighted workers in the service sector. Waiters and valets adored him. As fast as money came in from the music and the modeling contract, it went out even faster.

Men in Black's Will Smith once described how he became a man in the red with spending sprees that included flying to Tokyo on an impulse and buying every single item in a clothing store regardless of whether or not it fit. That's a typical symptom of compulsive shoppers, and there's even a twelve-step program devoted to the affliction. While not in Smith's megafortune financial league, in retrospect Wahlberg probably would have appreciated being told about the Imelda Marcos version of Alcoholics Anonymous.

"I didn't know where I was going, I was just going," he said. Mark was going *everywhere*—in grand style. "Bro, I was spending money as quick as I could make it. Clothes, rented jets, a boat, going to the Palm [an expensive West Hollywood restaurant] and ordering four-and-one-half-pound lobsters, leaving $500 tips at bars—man, my credit-card bills ran from $70,000 to $150,000 a month!"

These spending disasters would pale in comparison with Mark's next misstep—a potential career-killer that erupted at the same time his second album reached record stores and radio-station playlists.

But first, Mark had become such an important sociological phenomenon, his life had to be rendered in a full-length book.

CHAPTER 7

From Billboard to Coffee Table

Not many twenty-one-year-olds merit an autobiography. However, as 1991 turned into 1992, singles kept escaping from *Music for the People*, and their success kept Mark in the public eye and on countless magazine covers, invariably shirtless and ripped to shreds. The public, especially teenage girls, couldn't get enough of the gorgeous guy who talked tough but looked like a puppy dog. Okay, a puppy dog with sixteen-inch biceps.

Mark always catered to his fans. At the end of each concert, after the ritual pants-dropping, he would rush to the edge of the stage and stretch out his hands to the sea of girls who wanted to swim in the essence of Marky Mark. Like a bare-chested politician, Mark worked the crowd for all it was worth—a few hundred million bucks by now.

Magazine covers and interviews weren't enough to sate his fans, who couldn't get enough of the Wahlberg experience. Considerately, Mark decided to feed this hunger with an autobiography, titled simply, *Marky Mark*. HarperPerennial, a division of the prestigious publishing house HarperCollins, offered him a lucrative book deal and a co-author, celebrity photojournalist Lynn Goldsmith.

Donnie's helpful hand in the project is evident in the copyright. Although it's his brother's autobiography, the copyright holder is Donnie D. Productions, which a year later would produce Mark's workout video.

Indeed, the handsome coffee-table book was a family affair. It was Mark's life story, after all, and all the Wahlbergs contributed quotes about the most famous member of the family. Their affectionate comments provided the text for the photos which appear on every other page of this glossy trade paperback.

At first, *Marky Mark* seemed destined to perpetuate his bad-boy gangsta rapper image. The dedication contains the now infamous quote, "I wanna dedicate this book to my dick." The accompanying illustration shows Mark in Madonna mode, grabbing his crotch. This time, however, he wears a baggy denim windbreaker, unbuttoned to give just a peek at the famous chest and abdomen that led to temporary immortalization in Times Square and the Sunset Strip.

The title page provides more fleshploitation, with Mark doing a double biceps back pose. But the next page, an introduction by co-author Goldsmith, undercuts all the macho posturing. Goldsmith recalls meeting Mark four years earlier, before the Marky Mark phenomenon overwhelmed Mark Wahlberg, the shy teenager.

At nineteen, according to Goldsmith, he had been "a sorta skinny kid. Mark truly built himself up with hard work and discipline," Goldsmith wrote. Or, as Mark described himself, post-puberty and pre-gym he had just been "a little, pimple-faced ugly kid."

Marky Mark, like its subject, is a curious mix of the sacred and the profane. In a Q&A, Goldsmith asks, "Do you think you've changed in the last year?" Mark's answer: "Fuck yeah. My whole life has made a fuckin' 360-degree turn." (The teenage girls who lapped up his words of wisdom didn't even notice that a "360-degree turn" would have put Mark right back where he started, rather than at the top of the charts, where he was when his autobiography reached bookstores.)

Although the book is supposed to be about all things Marky, the star is generous in exposing his band members, whose personalities and quirks he describes with a familiarity that suggests they are more than just professional colleagues, more like confidants. A funky bunch of guys spills over a double-truck page spread: his record producer Marc Benesch, and the group members: Scottie Gee, Dick Scott, Hector, Andy, and DJ Terry.

Hector, Mark writes, is the band's Philosopher King. "He's into philosophy. He's always evaluating everything and studying and shit. And always likes to debate upon things. Between him, me, and [bodyguard] Boom, we always have a deep conversation about politics or religion or something like that."

You get the feeling that Mark doesn't talk politics with DJ Terry. "He's like the class clown, he's always getting into some ill shit. Crazy motherfucker. He loves to fuck. He's always out trying to make a porno movie," says Wahlberg.

When he describes Scott Gee, it's clear that there's room for only one hunky teen idol in the group. "He tries to be the pretty boy of the crew. I call him Leather Face, because his face looks like it's made out of leather. He looks like that guy from *Texas Chainsaw Massacre*."

But immediately after all this tough-guy talk, Mark prints the group prayer that precedes every performance, like a basketball team huddle just before hitting the court. "Dear Lord, we come to you tonight asking for your guidance, your strength, and your goodwill. Thank you for helping us all out, helping us to succeed in life. And for giving our family, friends, and loved ones your blessings. Deliver us to them safely. I will always pray in your name, and the name of the Father, the Son, and the Holy Spirit. Amen. Let's do it, y'all."

Mark has always had a spiritual side, which has grown as he has matured. He also consults with the family priest he has known since childhood.

It would take all his faith and spiritual underpinnings to cope with the misfortunes that awaited him.

CHAPTER 8

Near Career-Death Experiences

Nineteen ninety-three was not one of Mark Wahlberg's favorite years. With the possible exception of 1988 when he was doing time, 1993 had to be the worst of times.

His second album, *You Gotta Believe*, came out and dropped off the charts almost as soon as it landed. The boosterish *YM* magazine called it "red-hot," but apparently the reporter for the teen-zine had failed to read the music trades, which were cold about the album's artistic merit and its sales potential.

You Gotta Believe, which had a tougher, "street" sound than the gentle rap of his debut CD, entered *Billboard*'s Top 200 chart at number 67 on October 3, 1992. That was as high as it ever got. It fell off *Billboard*'s list fourteen weeks later on January 23, 1993, at number 198.

Somehow, the album also managed to land on *Billboard*'s R&B chart, although no one ever described Mark's style as rhythm-and-blues. *You Gotta Believe* entered that chart on December 26, 1992, but fell off the list three weeks later, having peaked at number 66.

While *Music for the People* had sold an impressive 1.4 million albums, *You Gotta Believe* sold a less-than-credible 218,000 units. Unlike his debut CD, which had spun off four hit singles, *You Gotta Believe's* title track sold only 163,000 units as a single, and his discouraged label decided not to release any more tracks.

Billboard gave the album a so-so review, but the critic's prediction about its commercial success turned out to be too optimistic: "Pop rapper eschews instant-recognition samples in favor of crossover-ready rhyming and production provided by his brother, New Kid on the Block [Donnie] Wahlberg. Siblings trade rhymes on 'Loungin',' while Donnie flies solo on 'American Dream,' a chronicle of two broken lives (one of them Mike Tyson's). Thought-provoking but never shocking, this album is bound to penetrate the mind of teens and playlists of Top 40 stations."

Reflecting perhaps its female readership's taste in music and cute guys, *Seventeen* magazine hailed Mark's new album as a work of "genius" and gave it a rave that practically amounted to a sales pitch. "Giving the gift of music this season is a cool way to impart instant emotion: You can turn your friends on, sweep them off their feet, or offer a comforting hug. More practically, you can prevent them from becoming the only schmo in school who doesn't own the new Marky Mark album. To avert such a social catastrophe, spring for *You Gotta Believe*, Mark's latest muscle-flexing work of genius. It's stoked with totally danceable hip-hop/house tracks, like the well-named 'Gonna Have a Good Time.'"

Billboard was dead wrong about the album reaching the Top 40, but it was correct about Mark's sway over teen fans. Another magazine described sales of the record as "only mediocre." But while girls didn't seem to want him on audio cassette or CD, they still wanted him onstage in the flesh.

In January 1993, *Entertainment Weekly* noted that the band toured "frenetically—Japan, France, New York, London, San Francisco in the last two months." The European press received his second album more warmly, which may explain the reason for the global tour. (Indeed, the international headquarters for the Marky Mark fan club was based in Amsterdam until recently.) *Hitkrant*, a Dutch magazine, called *You Gotta Believe* a "perfect combination for both dance floor and charts." Germany's *Pop Rock* said, "Marky presents himself a little harder, fresher and groovier on his second album. His specialty: cool raps and great chorus-arrangements."

In the United States, while fans didn't swarm to record stores to buy his second offering, thousands of teenage girls stormed a Manhattan bookstore to demand his autograph on his autobiography.

Girls and gays still adored Wahlberg, but professional tastemakers put Mark on the "Out" portion of their "In" and "Out" lists at the beginning of 1993. But those were cynical, sophisticated journalists. Marc Benesch, general manager of Mark's Interscope label, knew the power base that would continue to keep the rapper in the public eye, if not at the top of the charts. "The core audience still wants cute Mark," Benesch said in 1993, as *You Gotta Believe* tumbled off the music charts. "Whenever an artist breaks so big the first time around, the expectations are equally great. But the marketplace is always changing."

And so was the direction of Mark's career. Benesch correctly predicted that other media would welcome the intriguing young man long after music fans went on to the New Menudo on the Block. "Music is intertwined with TV and movies, and so are artists. It's not like five or ten years ago, when you had a musical career and that was it. Mark, I believe, has been blessed with a talent, whether it's music or TV or movies or all of them combined." Benesch must have owned a crystal ball. Within four years, Mark would be all over magazine covers again, but this time with his shirt on, and promoting a succession of major Hollywood films.

Lynn Goldsmith, who served as his biographer and "court photographer," urged Mark to branch out into other media since recording artists usually spend such a short time at the top, whereas actors have a shot at lifetime achievement awards after thirty years of steady employment.

Commenting on the poor showing of *You Gotta Believe*, Goldsmith said, "Obviously, Mark's record is not exactly burning up the charts. How many rap albums can you put out? I would be looking for projects for him in the avenue of entertainment. I would want him to take acting classes; he picked up working in front of the camera very quickly [for music videos]. The Wahlberg family has a lucky star over their house."

Some music-industry analysts felt Mark's ability to pack a stadium or bookstore reflected the continuing popularity of his first album. They predicted the fate of all one-hit wonders. Mark seemed destined to become the new Vanilla Ice: In yo' face today, out of yo' mind tomorrow. A white rapper who would have one big hit, then disappear into the "Whatever Happened to . . . ?" trivia category.

A British magazine begged to differ. The U.K.'s *Hit CD* magazine reported on Mark's follow-up album: "This is a meaty slice of firm and funky rocking rap which says that Marky Mark will be around for a while longer."

The magazine's prediction turned out to be true, but not in a way fans of the rapper's music might have guessed. Maybe not even Mark, who would have been surprised to know that his continued public recognition would be fueled by controversy as much as by popularity.

The apparent end of his rap career, however, was just the beginning of his nightmare that year. To promote an album few wanted to buy, Wahlberg made the rounds of TV and radio talk shows, even traveling to Europe to jigger sales. The chat shows became a nightmare of accusations and interrogations. One host asked how he felt about the fact that his body "sold" better than his new album.

Mark's description of the talk-show experience in a nutshell: "I was kind of pissed."

He came to regret one appearance in particular. In January 1993 on *The Word*, a TV talk/variety show in London, the performer had the misfortune to share a sofa, then the stage, with a reggae singer called Shabba Ranks, who used his appearance on the program as a platform to denounce gays and lesbians. In fact, "denounce" is too weak a word to describe Shabba's exhortation to his fans to go out and "shoot and kill" gays.

Other rappers have created a tough-guy image for themselves with similar suggestions about law enforcement officers, but at least cops are armed and can protect themselves against crazy fans who heed their idols' deadly orders.

Wahlberg, of course, didn't second Shabba's vicious instructions. In fact, he later claimed he hadn't been onstage when Shabba announced his jihad against homosexuals. It was only after he saw a videotape of the show that he realized he had been tainted by association. Wahlberg didn't know of Shabba's remarks when the reggae singer urged him to do a set together. A rapper, Mark didn't want to participate regardless of Ranks' political philosophy, and a tape reveals the two hosts of *The Word* shoving Wahlberg over into the performing area.

After their forced duet, the studio audience began to boo. Mark thought it was a critique of his performance, not Shabba's sentiments about gays. Mark was already in a foul mood because, at twenty-two, he was suffering a post-adolescent outbreak of acne. The U.K. host from hell urged him on the air to put some "Oxy on my face," Mark recalled a year later, still fuming.

Reacting to the boos, Mark screamed, "Fuck you! Fuck everybody! I can say whatever the hell I want. Shabba can say whatever the hell he wants. And you can say whatever the hell you want!" Then he slammed the microphone down and stomped off the set.

After he saw the video, Mark wished he had screamed at Shabba instead of the audience. The crack about his complexion was annoying. The videotape of Ranks was horrifying. Mark said, "I couldn't believe it happened. I had been sitting there like I was on *The Gong Show*. Then all this!"

A few months later Mark got his chance to tell Ranks what he wished he had said right after the talk show. When they met again at the Grammy Awards in the spring of 1993, Shabba apologized for causing Mark so much grief. Ranks told him, "There are certain people who say you've gotten into a lot of trouble out of what happened. I didn't mean to implicate you in it at all."

The apology was too little, too late, and nobody was there to witness it or help repair Mark's image as an unwitting homophobe. Mark let Shabba have it at the hotel they were both staying at during the Grammys. "What is *wrong* with you? Why would you say something like that?" Mark asked the reggae singer. Ranks' response: "Well, you know, I'm a man of the Bible." Ranks replayed his talk-show rant with more biblical quotations. Mark stopped the impromptu lecture. "Well, yo! If that's the way you feel, then that's the way you feel. But you don't have a right to be disrespecting people like that. First of all, you're not God, so you shouldn't be running around preaching things like that," Mark told Judy Weider in the January 25, 1994, issue of *The Advocate*.

Wahlberg knew he had a huge gay following in the states, perhaps worldwide, because of the Calvin Klein gig. Mark knew better than to bite the hands that fed money into the hands of record-store clerks selling his albums.

Guilt by association is no guilt at all, but try telling that to the Gay and Lesbian Alliance Against Defamation (GLAAD), which felt Wahlberg was guilty as hell of homophobia. The pressure group sent a letter to Calvin Klein, protesting his poster boy's tenuous affiliation with the politically incorrect Shabba. Other angry gays showed their feelings by sending anonymous packages filled with soiled underwear to Klein's pristine Manhattan headquarters.

Klein, who had hired Wahlberg as a model but did not represent him as spokesperson or manager, ignored GLAAD's letter. Klein didn't feel any responsibility for the behavior of an "outside contractor." Wahlberg, after all, was not an employee of the Klein empire, just a temp worker, albeit a magnificent one.

When Klein didn't respond to GLAAD's complaint, the organization threatened a massive demonstration at a location picture-perfect and camera-ready for the *Six o'Clock News*, *Hard Copy*, and half-hourly reruns on CNN's *Headline News*. Ground zero would be Times Square, right under Wahlberg's massive billboard.

The clothing magnate came to heel almost immediately and quickly issued a statement: "We at Calvin Klein in no way condone any act of violence, be it anti-racial, anti-homosexual, or crimes of any bias. I truly believe that the Mark Wahlberg we know today as Marky Mark is, in fact, a reformed young man who has grown way beyond his years as a result of a particularly difficult childhood."

Klein kowtowed, but while GLAAD was waiting for a similar apology from their real target, it decided to do a little research, aided by another group with an even bigger bone to pick, the Committee Against Anti-Asian Violence.

Although Wahlberg had been a major public figure for two years, no one in the entertainment press—notorious for its paranoia of being blacklisted by publicists who cut off journalists who tick them off for writing unflattering articles about their clients—had ever publicized Wahlberg's prison sentence for assaulting a Vietnamese man five years earlier. The Asian activists knew about the incident and were happy to share it with their gay brethren in the trenches.

GLAAD's publicity director, Donald Suggs, said, "[Wahlberg] has to admit that he's been involved in bias crime," referring to the assault, not the talk-show appearance, which was GLAAD's real beef with the rapper. But Mark's run-in with the Asian man and the law made better news and got more ink and TV time. "Because the biggest stereotype about bias crime is that it's just guys getting out of control. That's not what it is. It is systematically targeting members of a minority group for violence," Suggs said.

Wahlberg had not bashed gays, verbally or physically, and some felt GLAAD's protests were just grandstanding and publicity-seeking. But the group's get-tough attitude did serve as a warning to other would-be homophobes in the public eye: Bash us at your peril . . . and the potential ruination of your career. In the early 1990s, just how powerful such a boycott could be was demonstrated when a false rumor circulated that Donna Summer, gay men's favorite disco queen, had denounced her fans after becoming a born-again Christian.

In 1990, *New York* magazine quoted Summer as saying AIDS was a "divine ruling" against gays. Summer sued the magazine for $30 million and eventually settled out of court. But the damage had been done. Her label, Atlantic Records, treated her like damaged goods, and gay discos refused to spin her new albums, depriving her of invaluable exposure in a market known for setting trends—gay clubs.

Mark could have looked at Summer's precipitous fall as a warning on how *not* to manage your career. Soon, even legitimate publications like *US* magazine were reporting that Wahlberg had defended the "First Amendment rights of Shabba Ranks, who spouted anti-gay nonsense," when Mark had done nothing of the sort. The magazine also labeled Ranks' comments incorrectly when it called them "nonsense" instead of categorizing them as what they were, an incitement to kill homosexuals. Dangerous nonsense, indeed!

Negotiations between Wahlberg's manager, Dick Scott, and GLAAD and the Asian group took on the complexity of a SALT treaty. The negotiations were complex but also quick. Only a day after Klein apologized publicly for his model's less-than-model behavior, Mark issued this apology: "In 1986, I harassed a group of school kids on a field trip, many of them African-American. And in 1988, I assaulted two Vietnamese men over a case of beer. I used racist language during these encounters and people were seriously hurt by what I did," he said in a statement the Associated Press circulated worldwide on February 19, 1993. "I know there are kids out there doing the same stuff now and I just want to tell them, *don't do it.*"

Wahlberg did better than make verbal amends. He promised to appear in a public-service announcement denouncing bigotry in all forms, including gay-bashing: "I want to make it clear that I condemn anti-gay hatred and violence." GLAAD and the Committee Against Anti-Asian Violence were mollified and called off the planned demonstrations in Times Square.

Still the brilliant self-promoter, Wahlberg knew that actions speak louder than prepared statements released to news services. Three days before his written apology, he made a calculated appearance in the heart of the gay ghetto of West Hollywood at Book Soup, a classy bookstore on the Sunset Strip. Appearing there before his public apology hit the news wires took genuine courage. The purported reason was a book-signing for his coffee-table autobiography, *Marky Mark and the Funky Bunch*; the subtext, as actors like to say, was, *"See, I'm not a homophobe."*

Indeed, his charming behavior at Book Soup suggested he was a gay guy's best friend. A reporter from the *Los Angeles Times* noticed two very different demographics at the trendy bookshop: teenage Latinas and thirty-something white male homosexuals. "It's an incongruous demographic mix few, if any other pop stars can claim," the *Times* reporter wryly observed.

Indeed, Amanda Kragten, until recently the head of the Marky Mark fan club, agrees that the two groups like Mark, but focus their desire on different parts of his anatomy. "It seems there are two categories of 'typical' fans, if such a person exists," says

Amanda, who works as a school administrator in Amsterdam. "One are the teenage girls that like him for his looks, smile, and such. The other category is homosexual men, who basically like Mark for his body and muscles. The Calvin Klein ads are *very* popular [in Europe]."

At Book Soup, a Latina autograph-seeker resisted the urge to grab her idol, typical behavior of smash-and-grab fans. Clutching a copy of *Rolling Stone*, a magazine she never read until Mark appeared on the cover, the sixteenish girl said while waiting on line, "I'm *afraid* to touch him. He's so chiseled, I might get a paper cut!"

Although Wahlberg had not yet made his public apology, another autograph-seeker, Richard Noble, felt no apology was necessary. "He's doing important things," said Noble, a member of Coronation L.A., a gay-rights group. Noble mentioned the rap star's recent appearance at the gay disco Arena for an AIDS fund-raiser. The club has a large Latino transvestite following.

While Noble was a noted activist, the gravity of his endorsement of Wahlberg was undercut by the fact that in homage to his idol he showed up at the book signing wearing a leather jacket and underwear—and nothing else. Noble explained his outfit that evening: "I can feel his heart. And he's gorgeous, and he's got a beautiful body. I just wanted to come in my Calvin Kleins and show my support," reported Chris Willman in the *Los Angeles Times* (February 16, 1993).

The book-signing was designed to sell books. Some of his female fans, however, showed up with posters the *Los Angeles Times* speculated had been ripped off bus stops. "Hundreds of sheets of glass in public-transit shelters have died for his pecs," the newspaper said.

Wahlberg's bodyguard was not impressed by this vandalism even though it was for a good cause. "We can't sign CDs [or posters], baby," Boom, his outsized bodyguard, told one crestfallen teenage girl. However, Mark could and did. At several fans' requests, Wahlberg even autographed his crotch on the Klein posters. So much for selling books that night. Intuitively or maybe not, Wahlberg knew the autographed posters were selling something *else* just as important to career longevity. Or, as the *Times* said, "No one will admit to busting up a bus stop to get [a poster]; Marky's pecs could conceivably sag before the statute of limitations runs out."

Mark Wahlberg became Everystud to gay fans, whom he continued to actively court. At a formal fund-raiser for AIDS Project Los Angeles, attended by Hollywood heavyweights like Barry Diller, David Geffen, and superstar manager Sandy Gallin, Wahlberg volunteered to participate as a runway model in a fashion show honoring his original benefactor, Calvin Klein.

Pictures from the event show the flitterati in haute couture and white tie at the June 1993 gala (held at the stadium-sized Hollywood Bowl)—except for Mark, who is wearing jeans which have fallen to ankle level. He's also shirtless. And showing zero-percent body fat.

With no exaggeration, *US* magazine said, "Rapper Marky Mark stole the show by dropping his jeans." *US* also mentioned he grabbed "his privates" on the runway.

The *L.A. Weekly* added details celebrity-friendly magazines like *US* had omitted. Tongue practically gouging a hole in cheek, the *Weekly* reported that during the finale "the unmistakable Marky Mark . . . dropped his pants and grabbed his crotch to Martin Luther King's 'I Have a Dream' speech. The crotch-grabbing was particularly effective on the giant video screen that projected the show to the rear seats."

A very long home videotape of the runway performance confirms the *Weekly*'s account. The videocam operator zooms in on Wahlberg's underwear. Mark's fist encircles the head of his penis.

Michael Anketell, executive chairman and producer of the gala, found Mark a dream to work with, but considered Mark's behavior inappropriate at an event to raise funds for a fatal, sexually transmitted disease. "He just pulled his pants down," Anketell erroneously told me. The tape shows Mark's pants falling down on their own as he struts along the ramp. The rest of Anketell's account jibes with the tape he gave me. "He started grabbing a rather large basket. He definitely had some 'wood' going on there. He was getting off on it, I think.

"AIDS has everything to do with safe sex. Underwear is one thing. It was real sexy the way it was done, some guys ripping off their shirts, which they weren't supposed to do, but they did anyway. But I felt he was crossing the line at a black-tie event, especially when I saw him semi-hard," Anketell told me.

Anketell has a photo of Mark standing onstage in front of Barbara Davis (the wife of oil billionaire Marvin Davis) in the audience. Unlike Anketell, Mrs. Davis wasn't grossed out by the kid standing at, uh, attention in front of her. "She has a *big* smile on her face," Anketell said.

Hey, it was for a good cause, and the gala did raise $1.3 million for the chronically cash-strapped AIDS Project Los Angeles, although published figures say forty percent of the money went to the overpriced, overproduced gala, which included the cost of flying in Klein's personal hairdresser from London at APLA's expense, according to Anketell.

Klein had personally asked Wahlberg to strut his stuff at the event but took no credit for his protégé's choice of, uh, choreography on the runway. "Marky Mark was wearing my underwear and taking off his jeans in concert long before I discovered him. So this is about honesty and the truth," Klein said rather cryptically.

A close examination of the runway tape speaks volumes about Wahlberg's by-then deteriorating relationship with the clothing mogul. At the end of the fashion show, Klein appears onstage and Mark looks at his "boss" with an adoring gaze. Klein completely ignores him and doesn't even make eye contact. Klein's long acceptance speech thanks a laundry list of participants who donated their time to the high-profile fund-raiser, but the fashion mogul doesn't mention Wahlberg by name. After the rambling speech, Klein motions to the 350 other models to follow him down the runway for one last stroll. He moves toward Mark as though he's finally going to acknowledge him. Instead, he gestures to another model standing next to Wahlberg, then wraps his arm around the other star fashion plate and Klein spokesmodel, Kate Moss. The two lead the parade together and Mark follows behind.

Klein's public stiffing of the youth who had made his sales jump thirty-seven percent lends credibility to the Klein executive who told me Wahlberg's contract was not renewed at this time because the magnate feared Mark's alleged homophobia would rub off on his underwear.

Backstage, however, the hands-off policy disappeared. According to Mike Anketell, who joined the show's participants there, the powerful gay claque known as the Velvet Mafia swarmed around the shirtless Wahlberg. It was definitely a touchy-feely moment. Anketell told me that David Geffen, Klein, and Barry Diller "were enthralled" to be in the presence of the twenty-two-year-old boy from Boston's inner city. "They just sort of encircled him backstage. He was Calvin's boy and man of the hour. They couldn't congratulate him or touch him or have their photograph taken with him enough times. They just kept touching him, putting their arms around him. Pulling and tugging at him. Nothing inappropriate," Anketell added. "*There were too many photographers there.*"

A record-label executive and movie producer, Geffen is the richest man in Hollywood, with a personal fortune worth $2 billion. Barry Diller is probably the most influential man in the history of television, creating the miniseries format and the Fox network when he wasn't turning tacky cable shopping channels into the Tiffany's of interactive TV.

And yet these two moguls found themselves being stiff-armed by the ferociously heterosexual Wahlberg. Anketell said, "Mark is very straight and very conscious when he's around somebody who's gay. It's like, 'You keep your distance and shake hands.'" When Geffen and Diller tried to hug Mark, Anketell said, "He was pulling away as much as they were tugging at him."

Wahlberg, however, knew who had made him a national icon, and he didn't rebuff the maker of his fortune, despite the public snub on the runway. "The only one he'd really let hug him was Calvin," Anketell told me over a pot of herbal tea at the Silver Spoon restaurant in West Hollywood on March 30, 1998.

With a single phone call, Geffen or Diller can make or break a career. Why would they engage in such pushy behavior with a straight guy?

Anketell, who witnessed the incident, theorized it was about domination, not sex. "I think it was a power thing. '*We're* more powerful than you are. *You're* Marky Mark. *I'm* David Geffen. *I'm* Barry Diller. You'll do what I want you to do.'"

Not backstage. "Mark is his own guy. He's a street kid and he's a wise-ass," Anketell said. After the show, Mark and others retired to their favorite club hangout, the Roxbury on the Sunset Strip. Anketell said, "When I saw him at the Roxbury later that evening, he was with the prettiest girls there . . . models who had been in the show."

By now, Wahlberg seemed to realize his underexposure was beginning to amount to overexposure. "When I saw Calvin and all dem in tuxes I thought, 'Whoa, I *am* underdressed,'" as *Premiere* magazine misquoted him. Despite a lack of formal education, Wahlberg is simply not a "*deze*, *dem*, and *doze*" kind of guy. Anketell agreed with me that the *Premiere* quote was a grotesque rendering of his speech patterns. "He was very articulate," Anketell said.

Wahlberg shouldn't have felt underdressed, however, compared to the outfits of the other runway models. *US* reported that "topless teenaged girls and boys in jockstraps" also hit the ramp at the fund-raiser.

US exaggerated. Again, a close inspection of the tape shows at least a dozen topless guys on the runway, but nothing you wouldn't see at the beach, though bizarre at a gilt gala where the audience is in black ties and tuxedos. Only two female models went topless at the function. One covered her breasts with her hands, nothing more shocking than what you might see on the cover of *Vanity Fair* when actress Demi Moore is feeling particularly frisky. However, the other female appeared topless and kept *her* hands at her sides. Both models looked much older than teenagers.

With a public apology and several well-publicized public appearances in the homosexual heartland, Wahlberg had stopped a public fistfight before anyone's hands were even raised in protest. Besides the trip to the Hollywood Bowl and the book-signing at Book Soup, Wahlberg showed up at Mickey's, a gay disco on Santa Monica Boulevard in West Hollywood, later that summer. "I think Mark was on a mission to dispel that whole homophobic thing that was going around about him. He made it a point to welcome the audience [at Mickey's] and tell them how much he loved them. It was his management or his publicist saying, 'You've got to really clean this up. . . .'" Anketell said.

Anketell's final take on Mark's real feelings about gays: Wahlberg is not homophobic, but he feels uncomfortable around gay men. Before the show, to calm stage fright (or perhaps his fear of homosexuals), Mark, Kate Moss, and Anketell shared a marijuana cigarette and sipped champagne. After a few tokes, producer Anketell went to check the audience. Mark and Kate continued to toke. "He got a little high backstage on marijuana and champagne [to] loosen himself up a bit. He does a lot of pot," says Anketell. Wahlberg was generous and brought his own stash. "It was good stuff," Anketell added.

By the time Wahlberg hit the runway, he was "pretty zonked," according to Anketell.

A former fashion publicist, Anketell has worked with demanding, temperamental celebrities from hell. Wahlberg was none of these things, according to Anketell. "I found him to be a really down-to-earth, nice guy. He could not have been nicer. He knew what he was there to do. His heart was in it. He really cared about the cause. He was a sweetheart, very kind, very gentle, very, you know, 'What do you want me to do?' I didn't find him pretentious, not like Kate. She was totally the opposite of him. He seems like somebody who remembers where he came from. There's something very humble about him. He was shy, like a straight guy."

In fact, his only "temperamental demand" had to do with his shyness, not a sense of entitlement. The other 300-plus models were amateurs and they all dressed—and undressed—together in the cavernous backstage area. As soon as he arrived at the Hollywood Bowl, Wahlberg scoped out the situation and demanded a separate dressing room, which was jerry-rigged with hanging sheets for privacy.

Most of the other models, Anketell believed, were gay, and Mark felt uncomfortable disrobing under the gaze of admirers of the same sex. "It was a gay thing. I really found him sort of clinging to the [female] models there like Kate Moss. He really wanted everybody to know without saying it that he was straight."

Still, Wahlberg, whom Anketell agrees is an exhibitionist, enjoyed the attention onstage in front of a largely gay audience. "He was enjoying it. He was getting off on the fact that the audience was eighty-five-percent gay men. You'll see it on the tape. He was enjoying himself, having a good time."

While the gay community welcomed Mark back after so much contrition, quietly, behind the scenes, Calvin Klein had made the decision to dump the controversial spokesmodel. Klein knew that gays bought his underwear and other products in disproportionate numbers, and no matter how much Wahlberg showed off his bottom to induce gay customers to buy Klein's stuff, Klein kept his eye on the bottom line.

Despite Mark's public apologies, despite his drawer-dropping appearance at an AIDS benefit to honor Klein, despite the "Howdy, guys!" at Mickey's, the clothing magnate decided Wahlberg was more trouble than he was worth. A mid-level executive at Klein's New York headquarters told me, "Calvin dumped Marky because he made a lot of stupid, homophobic comments. It was bad for business. We couldn't get [Mark] to shut up. That was my impression. I know he was saying dumb things. I know perfectly well when we have someone who represents Calvin, we're very interested in the quality of the spokesperson's public utterances. Calvin engages in intense negotiations with potential models [about what they will say in public.]"

Officially, though, it was a mutual love affair between the fashion emperor and the famous boy who wore his new clothes. Neil Kraft, Klein's creative director during Mark's billboard reign, gave the young man high marks for dogged professionalism and punctuality. "He showed up on time and worked like a dog. He's a complete professional," Kraft said in 1992.

An item in the August 23, 1993, issue of *Time* magazine bears out the other executive's claim that Klein dropped Wahlberg. In the magazine's "Winners & Losers" column, Mark makes the top of the list of Losers: "Marky Mark. Calvin Klein said to be looking for new underpants pitchman." *Time* didn't say why, and the item would seem inexplicable since Wahlberg's participation had made underwear sales soar after he had donned a pair.

According to Wahlberg, it was a mutual parting of ways, with Mark perhaps being happier to leave than Klein was to let his best-selling salesman go. Mark was dissatisfied toward the end of the relationship. "I think the second campaign wasn't half as good as the first one or even necessary, because the first one did it. I don't want to be a Calvin Klein model forever. Nothing lasts forever."

Mark had the last word—actually the final image—on the end of the Klein affair. A visitor to his hotel suite in 1998 noticed a pair of underwear on the bathroom floor. The label said TOMMY HILFIGER.

Mark rejected the theory that activist groups exerted pressure on the powerful clothing mogul. GLAAD did not get him dumped, Wahlberg said in an interview with *The Advocate*. "The contract was always over in December," he said in late 1993.

The Calvin Klein executive who spoke to me added that the company's current poster stud, Antonio Sabato Jr.—who, coincidentally, costarred with Wahlberg in *The Big Hit* (1998)—has been a dream to work with. And Sabato knows better than to tick off an important demographic. "Antonio doesn't say stupid things about gay guys who worship him and ogle his posters," the executive told me.

Soon Mark would confront an opponent considerably scarier than angry Asians, irate gays, or a billionaire bootywear magnate. In a battle one pundit called "dueling icons," Marky Mark took on Madonna and found himself getting roughed up by her men toys.

CHAPTER 9

Mano a Mano with Madonna

In the summer of 1993, six months after he had averted a riot in Times Square by outraged Asians and gays, Mark found himself going mano a mano with Madonna at a party in the Hollywood Hills. The guests were A-list, with the A also standing for Attitude. It was hosted by Gerry Harrington, a high-profile actors' manager, and his wife, Angela Janklow, a sometime journalist better known as the daughter of super-literary agent Richard Janklow.

Among the A-list, the biggest *A*'s—and you can interpret *A* any way you want to—had to be Madonna and Mark. What happened that sultry July evening has more conflicting versions than the Lewinsky/Tripp/Clinton depositions (although the amusing distortions in the supermarket tabloids seem more like hallucinations than reportage).

We do know this. The event celebrated the twenty-ninth birthday of super-hot Alek Keshishian, who directed Madonna's concert film, *Truth or Dare* (1991), the most commercially successful documentary ever made, topping even *Woodstock* (1970) and *Marjoe* (1972).

According to *People* magazine, Madonna picked the fight, telling Mark, "You're not my friend." Madonna was angry because Wahlberg had made some unflattering comparisons between her and a famous movie ghoul. In a February 1993 cover story, *YM* magazine had quoted Mark's first impression of the Material Omnivore. "Man, she's cool, you know? She does her thing." Then he contradicted what he had just said. "But there was something about her that just disappointed me. First of all, I thought she was fly. I mean, she's very smart, she's very controversial. But then I see her, and she's got this gold tooth in her mouth and all this shit around her eyes. She looked like Beetlejuice or something. But you know, she seemed like a nice person."

No one has ever called Madonna a conventional beauty, but for those who haven't seen the title character in *Beetlejuice* (1988), Michael Keaton plays a demon with snakes for hair and flesh rotting off his bones.

The *New York Daily News*, a family newspaper which publishes stories like "Headless Body Found in Topless Bar," had to rely on euphemisms to report the stars' argument after Madonna heard about the *YM* interview. The paper reported the singer and the rapper exchanged "sexually explicit insults."

This is not a family book, however. According to the January 25, 1994, issue of *The Advocate*, both stars exchanged "Fuck yous."

Mark spotted comedian Rosie O'Donnell, Madonna's best gal pal, at the party and said hello, then ducked into the bathroom. He suspected O'Donnell must have "told on him," because when he emerged from the loo, the pop star was waiting for him right outside the door.

"Madonna came trucking down the hallway with combat boots on. When she saw me, she came up to me and started going crazy," Mark recalled for the January 25, 1994, issue of *The Advocate*.

Lamely he asked, "What's up, Madonna?"

His recollection of her response: "Don't fucking say hi to me. You know what the fuck you fucking did. You dissed me. You're a fucking asshole, a fucking fake."

Mark tried to explain that *YM* had quoted him out of context when he'd compared her to Michael Keaton's rotting demon. "Well, first of all, Madonna, it wasn't what it was supposed to be," he said about the misquote.

Madonna replied, "Well, fuck you!"

Mark said, "Well, fuck you too!"

Then, according to Wahlberg (in *The Advocate* article), Madonna allegedly made a physical threat. "She said, 'Well, I'm going to get somebody to kick your ass.'"

Nightclub owner John Enos, an unidentified reggae artist (not Shabba!), and an executive with Madonna's Maverick record label, Steve Oseary, responded to Madonna's 911. They confronted Wahlberg at the party and said, "This ain't Boston. This is L.A."

Then the men displayed behavior that was much more typical of inner-city Boston than the rarified hills of Hollywood, "insinuating that they had a gun, trying to egg me on," Mark said. A veteran of much meaner streets than Sunset Plaza Drive in the Hollywood Hills, Mark dismissed these white collar thugs. "I was laughing at them, blowing it off!"

Wahlberg turned away and began to chat with a film-production executive from TriStar when Oseary and another Maverick label employee repeated the threats, according to Mark (in that same *Advocate* account). Wahlberg refused to be provoked and said, "As you can see, I just came here to have a good time."

The TriStar executive was amused and asked Mark, "What's *his* problem?"

Mark said to *The Advocate* that Oseary and the other record exec invited him to "step outside." When Mark demurred again, one of his antagonists allegedly said, "I know you don't want to fight me. I knew you was a pussy."

Dem's fighting words for a boy from Dorchester, and Mark accepted their invitation. As they exited the house, another unidentified guest came up and said, "Yo, you and my man could just go one-on-one and squash it all now."

Mystified, Mark said, "What are you talking about?"

The "kid," as Mark described him in the *Advocate* account, responded by "grazing me on the side of the head."

Time magazine (August 16, 1993), which rarely covers celebrity brawling, claimed the kid only "shoved" Wahlberg. According to Mark, he hit the young man so hard he fell to the ground. Mark then leaped on top of him, but another partygoer hit the rap artist on the back of the head. Mark fell on the floor, and the wrestling match continued. A new combatant joined the fray and kicked Mark in the head.

The host, Gerry Harrington, screamed, "Take it outside." Which they did, according to *Time* magazine.

Just as the men left, Madonna, who had stayed indoors, couldn't resist saying good-bye to Mark. "Get the fuck out of here. You're a fucking asshole. I told you you were going to get your ass kicked."

Mark said simply, elegantly, "Oh, fuck you."

People magazine (August 16, 1993) called the fight outside the house a "semi-rumble," although it sounds more like assault and battery. Mark allegedly punched Oseary in the nose. Liz Rosenberg, Madonna's publicist, said, "[Oseary] will probably press charges. I think Marky broke his nose."

Rosenberg really earned her $1,000-a-week fee as Madonna's flack when she added a lethal tidbit about her client's antagonist. She informed *People* that Wahlberg had started the fight, not Madonna, when he called a member of her entourage a "homo." *Time* also repeated the accusation, but got this denial from Wahlberg: "I'm offended anyone would say that when I'm out there breaking boundaries."

Another rumor, reported in *The Advocate*, had Madonna miffed because Wahlberg had called her brother a "faggot." Mark denied that accusation in a January 1994 interview with the magazine. He also insisted that he didn't participate in the fight that had ensued once they left the party. "A big guy," Madonna's boyfriend, Mark said, followed him outside and began screaming. Mark ignored him, and the man started punching somebody else out. "I was like, 'I'm out of here.'"

Mark had an early audition the next morning, and he didn't want to be late—or show up with a damaged face!

The *Star*'s columnist, Janet Charlton, didn't attend the party, but her account was a lot more fun than *People*'s rendition. *People* had called the fracas a "semi-rumble." *Time* said "beer bottles were flying in a poolside melee." The *Star* had the stars "running for cover after Madonna triggered a free-for-all brawl." Madonna was the Trigger Girl that evening because Mark had "spurned her advances" and said she looked like Beetlejuice, according to the *Star*, which also "reported" that Madonna said to Wahlberg, "What are you doing here?" He said, "Get outta my face. I was invited to this party." Then Madonna called for backup from the executive suite, Maverick's Oseary, who hit Mark on the head with a coffee cup so hard that it shattered, per the *Star*.

At this point, the fight turned into a supposed knock-down brawl, involving such party guests as k.d. lang and Rosie O'Donnell! Additional likely participants listed in the tabloid account included Christian Slater, Joe Pesci, and Ethan Hawke. Like the tabs, the magazine loves a morality play with clearly defined good and bad guys. Madonna was the fall girl this time. When Mark tried to disengage from the fight, Madonna inflamed the situation and said, "Get your ass home, you little punk." Mark called her a "bitch and worse," although the magazine was too embarrassed to elaborate. John Enos, whom the *Star* called her boyfriend but whom *People* only identified as a nightclub impresario, decided to defend his lady. Enos, Mark, and their "posses ended up rolling on the ground kicking and punching," the *Star* said.

The hapless hosts, Gerry and Angela Harrington, saw their garden demolished, but they wouldn't have to worry about landscaping bills. Again, in good guy-bad girl storytelling, the *Star* reported that Mark apologized to the Harringtons and promised to pay for the bushes. While this was going on, "Madonna peeked through the fence."

Although the tabloid's account sounds downright comical, in retrospect, the accusations could have killed Wahlberg's show-business career (especially in light of the alleged anti-gay remarks). There's something about seeing a "fact" in print that lends it credibility.

For all its media sophistication and manipulation, the Gay and Lesbian Alliance Against Defamation apparently felt there was some truth in the *Star*'s narrative, although none of the mainstream press mentioned any homophobic outburst by Wahlberg. After the "semi-rumble" or "free-for-all brawl" or whatever actually happened that evening in the hills above Los Angeles, a spokesman for GLAAD said that a planned public-service announcement by Wahlberg in conjunction with the organization had been put "on hold until we verify what happened."

Ironically, the gay press was more forgiving—or perhaps more dismissive—than GLAAD was of the episode. Several magazines served as unofficial apologists. *Detour*, which sometimes seems to be the unofficial Marky Mark fan club newsletter, said in a 1997 Q&A with Wahlberg: "You didn't say anything anti-gay, but still you got branded homophobic. I thought everyone turned on you and it was unfair. I thought you got a bum rap," interviewer Dale Brasel wrote. *Out* magazine pooh-poohed his homophobia as "youthful insensitivity. . . . Whatever the ruckus, his charm and undeniable force of will have gotten him through it." *Interview* magazine also offered absolution, although nowhere in my search of published articles had Wahlberg ever done anything deserving absolution from the gay community. Even so, *Interview* said, "True, it didn't help that a few comments by Wahlberg, especially about gays, did not qualify him as Fulbright material, but they were more about lack of awareness than sagacity."

There was no need to forgive or dismiss anything Wahlberg had said *publicly* about homosexuals. He may still be studying for his GED, but Mark Wahlberg is very, very street-smart. Dissing or "dishing" or calling Madonna's boy toys "homos" is street-stupid and tantamount to career suicide. A young man clever enough to transform himself from striptease artist to serious artiste is way too savvy to expose himself in public in that way. Dropping your drawers will give you a gay following. Dropping your guard and saying what you really feel in public can turn your followers into leaders of a lynch mob in Times Square.

Jeff Yarbrough, who was editor-in-chief of *The Advocate* in November 1993 when Wahlberg did an interview for a cover story that ran in January the next year, also dismissed any alleged anti-gay slurs as a youthful mistake, and one for which Wahlberg was happy to make amends. "We asked him what went on . . . if indeed he did say something [homophobic] on the [British] talk show," Yarbrough told me.

Wahlberg insisted he had not. But if he had, Yarbrough and *The Advocate*'s readership were willing to forgive and forget. "Someone who is very young and who hasn't had a huge career in front of the public—they don't understand that if they make a remark it can truly be a lifelong situation they have to battle. If he did say something [against gays], sincere or not, he realized he had to straighten it out. He realized it was a mistake and wanted to rectify it by getting the word out," Yarbrough said.

Yarbrough also believes Wahlberg succeeded in his goal. "In retrospect, it did exactly what he wanted it to do. From then on, it was never brought up again in any formal or informal way. [The interview] completely quelled any anti-Marky Mark swell in the gay community.

"It was just effectively dropped after that story."

When he thought no one was officially listening, however, Wahlberg undercut his carefully-crafted gay-friendly image that he presented to the public and the media.

A mutual friend told me that privately Wahlberg has a more equivocal attitude toward gays. Our friend, who is straight, has a lot of gay buddies at Gold's Gym in Hollywood. One day at the gym, Wahlberg asked his friend, "Why do you hang out with *those* guys?" The friend, who agreed to the interview on condition of anonymity, says Wahlberg didn't use a homophobic term or even identify "those guys" as gay, but both men knew exactly what he meant. The friend, a personal trainer, told Mark, "I work with them. Ninety percent of the guys who work out here are gay." The trainer felt Wahlberg was giving him a hard time for fun, not harassment. "He was just giving me shit. That's just his thuggish personality coming out. He was teasing rather than being homophobic. The guys he mentioned, however, *were* very feminine."

That conversation occurred in 1997. Years earlier, Wahlberg hadn't taken such a lighthearted attitude toward gays. He confessed to this same friend that when he was much younger he had beat up a man simply because he was gay. Although Wahlberg had been accused of making homophobic comments, no one in the press had claimed actual assault.

In 1997, when he confided in his friend, Mark felt terrible about the incident from his wild youth. "When he was a lot younger," the mutual friend told me, "Mark felt he wasn't as tolerant, and now he is. He did tell me he beat up a guy because he was gay a long time ago. He was pretty young. There was some remorse there. He told me, 'I couldn't believe I did that just because of a guy's sexual preference!'"

Mark hasn't completely escaped past prejudices. A good friend of Wahlberg's felt hurt when Wahlberg saw him at the gym and Wahlberg made a gesture that seemed to mock his sexual orientation, however gently. An openly gay actor, this friend had never felt

Mark was homophobic before. Wahlberg knew the actor was gay and made a point of saying hi and chatting whenever they met at the gym. In fact, the generous star had even tried to get him a job on his film *Fear* (1996). It didn't work out, but the pal was grateful that the busy star had taken the time to buttonhole the director for an audition. But then one day, as the actor was leaving Gold's, Mark waved at him and said, "Hi, there!" The friend said Mark used an effeminate voice and "waved his hand sort of funny," in a fey gesture he described as "twinkle fingers!" Not a limp wrist by any means, but not "gimme five, mah man," either, said the actor.

"I felt kind of sad that someone would make fun of me," the up-and-coming actor said. The men had been close enough for Mark to have invited him to his house in the Hollywood Hills on more than half a dozen occasions.

The friend conceded that Wahlberg teased him about a lot of things, but the gay gesture left him perplexed. "Sometimes he makes fun of me, but he's been pretty nice. He makes a conscious effort to say hello, which is kind of strange. I found it strange when he made that gay comment to me because here I am just a struggling actor who's gay. Why is he picking on me? He'd like just come of this huge movie [*Boogie Nights*]. Did he want to make himself feel good? It just didn't make any sense."

The actor was distraught enough, that as Mark drove off in his Jeep he said to him, "Did you see the moon out?" He was about to drop his pants and moon Wahlberg. Mark Basile, Wahlberg's roommate, was in the car, however, and gave the actor a ferocious stare that seemed to say, "Don't even think of it!" The chastened actor kept his pants on.

Gold's Gym in Hollywood is like the Studio 54 of the 1990s, a place where gays and straights mingle comfortably. Although fearsome straight guys with prison tattoos and the physiques of competitive bodybuilders train there, Gold's has a large gay membership and the management caters to it. Gay magazines overflow bins inside and outside the two-story structure off Santa Monica Boulevard. Explicit posters of semi-nude men promoting gay special events called "circuit parties" adorn bulletin boards and the walls behind the water fountains on the first and second floors.

A poster for a circuit party called "Hooker" particularly grossed out Mark once, when he used the water fountain and saw a picture of a bare-chested guy on the wall. According to a friend, Wahlberg objected to the model's mediocre body, as well as the blatant nature of the poster and the title of the circuit party.

His friend also told me, "Mark would be like, 'What the heck is going on with this gym? Okay, I have nothing against anybody that's gay, but this is like turning into a gay nightclub!'"

The friend explained to Wahlberg that the poster was part of the gym's marketing strategy, since in his estimate, ninety percent of the membership was gay. The friend, whose muscular development matches Wahlberg's, said about the poster model, "He didn't have a great body. He didn't [look] like he ever worked out in a gym."

So what was Mark's problem—the blatantly gay poster or the pudgy poster boy?

"I think both," the pal decided.

For public consumption, Wahlberg gratefully accepts admiration and adoration from all demographics. Asked how he feels about his huge gay and "*mature* straight women" following, he said, "I think it's an honor. You know, gay men are not my preference so I'm not as excited as I am about the older-women part of it, but people have their likes and dislikes and I respect everybody for that and if I make people happy and entertain them, then cool.

"But I don't suck dick."

Not that he objected to anyone who did. Mark proudly mentions an openly gay uncle, his stepfather's brother, actually, who lived with the Wahlbergs for more than three years. He made it clear to his "stepuncle" that gay was okay with him. "I was always telling him, 'You gotta be yourself and do what you gotta do.'"

The uncle was a family favorite with a great fashion sense and a killer cookie recipe. "He made the best chocolate-chip cookies ever! He still spends Christmas with us. Christmastime, I'm telling you, you gotta come over!" Mark told the editor of *The Advocate*, Judy Wieder. "He buys us the best Christmas gifts. Fly shirts and sweaters! I'm talking *fashion*!"

Nineteen ninety-three definitely was not Mark's favorite year. Perhaps the only bright spot at the time was the glimmer of a career change for the troubled artist. In September 1993, Mark had a small supporting role in *The Substitute*, a cable-TV movie for the USA network, about a high-school teacher who has sex with a student. Mark wasn't the lucky student. He played a "punky classmate," per *TV Guide*, who blackmails the teacher. It was a minor part on a minor network, but then again Tom Cruise had been rejected for a role in a TV series based on the movie *Fame* (1980) because the casting director felt he wasn't "pretty enough."

The Substitute may have been his first big—okay, *medium*—break, but in retrospect, he has distanced himself from his first professional acting role. Criticism of the TV movie rattled him, and years later he said, "Somebody busted me for it yesterday, saying, 'I saw some movie where your throat gets sliced by a bottle.' I said, 'Wasn't me. That was Marky Mark, okay?' It was a big-money offer of two days' work on a script I didn't even read. I said the lines like I was onstage at one of my concerts, only wearing other funny clothes. When I was leaving, the director told me, 'You're going to win an award for this.'"

Despite his distaste for the screen material, Wahlberg knew enough not to bite the hand that might later feed him better lines. He told the director, "Oh, yeah? Thank you very much. I appreciate it."

That was in 1993. Three years later, as his feature-film career took off, Mark dismissed *The Substitute* as a "piece of shit" TV movie. And in retrospect, the "quick money" for two days' work wasn't quick enough for the fast-track star. "I probably got like a hundred grand for it—quick money. But it wasn't as quick as going out onstage and pulling down my pants. Man, that's where the big bucks is at."

Less than a year later, his striptease fee would also seem puny when he began to earn $2.5 million per feature film, although a movie shoot would take a bit longer than dropping his trousers at the end of a rap concert.

Cable TV wasn't the only small screen on which Wahlberg appeared in 1993. The most famous torso of the time decided to share his bodybuilding secrets on video. Calvin Klein and a host of magazines had made millions off his pecs, and the brilliant marketeer decided he wanted a piece of his pie, too.

CHAPTER 10

Making a Pec-tacle of Himself

These days, it seems every star has put out a workout video, no matter how unqualified, with the exception of Roseanne and the late John Candy.

At least Wahlberg *looked* qualified to dispense workout and diet tips when he starred in *The Marky Mark Workout: Form, Focus, Fitness* in 1993. Once again, Donnie provided the brains for his brother's splendid brawn. Big brother served as executive producer of the seventy-minute homage to physical perfection. Donnie also composed and produced the music without Mark's collaboration. (At least, Mark wasn't credited on the liner notes of the soundtrack.)

The video was indeed a family affair. Besides Donnie behind the camera as executive producer, their cousin, trainer Rich Minzer, appears on-camera and provides voiceovers, describing proper form as Mark demonstrates it. Scott Kalvert, who directed Wahlberg's music videos, and would later tap him for a pivotal movie role when Kalvert made his feature-film debut, directed the workout video.

Mark looks smashing. One critic, however, scoffed that the video seemed more of an excuse to show off the magnificent Mark than to provide instructions on how to look like him.

Mark begins the video with this self-confident manifesto to all those who want to be like him: "Listen up! If you want to look sharp and feel good, you got to get with the program. And now, you can spend a full day with me [actually, only seventy minutes] and some top trainers. We give you the form, the focus, and the facts. Remember, no matter where you're starting from or what you're looking for, this is the total package to get you there."

The video is divided into three segments: a home workout shot in the living room of an airy, light-filled mansion; a trip to Gold's Gym in Venice, California, the Mecca of muscle; and a ten-minute discussion on nutrition.

The home workout revolves around two wooden chairs and two dumbbells, minimum equipment for a maximum workout. Early on, Mark rips off his shirt with the excuse, "Can't do no abs with my shirt on, so . . ." He keeps it off for the rest of the video, even when he's demonstrating leg exercises and stretches, although he does wear long pants throughout.

When he removes his shirt, it appears his torso has been pre-oiled, since he's had no chance to work up a sweat so early on in the video.

To attract male viewers, Mark exercises on-camera with several beautiful women with bods as good as his. He calls them his "fly honeys."

During the home workout, he has only one female companion, who hoists lighter dumbbells, but duplicates his routine. Mark flirts with the woman throughout the workout, but gently and not in a harassing manner. In fact, most of the flirting consists of raising his eyebrows and suggesting the unspoken thought, *"Can you believe this babe?"*

After a few dumbbell kickbacks to develop the triceps portion of the arm, Mark appears visibly winded. He says, "I gotta take a break." When the video was made in 1993, a colleague said, "He smoked cigarettes constantly," which may explain the need for a break.

Amazingly, the next portion of the video didn't end up on the cutting-room floor. He may be tired, but his workout partner, the anorexic Amazon, looks as though she could still go a few rounds with Mike Tyson. She spontaneously offers to trade her lighter dumbbell for his! Mark frowns and his body stiffens as he silently rejects the offer. You wonder how his garrulous body language made it into the final cut.

The second segment moves to Gold's Gym. The video has several interesting self-revelations that speak volumes about his self-image, which isn't as self-confident as his public persona. He admits that when he first began working out at the Venice gym, home to major-name bodybuilders, he felt intimidated by the bigger guys.

Mark is shirtless at the gym, which is strictly forbidden even for other, less stellar members. Still basted in baby oil, Mark reclines on sophisticated apparatus called Smith machines without placing a towel on them—again, verboten at Gold's. Soon, inexplicably, Mark jump-cuts to a soundstage dressed to look like a gym. No further reference is made to Gold's. (Maybe management asked him to leave for greasing up the expensive equipment.)

Mark says in his opening manifesto that the workouts "are perfect for everybody—beginner or experienced," although knowledgeable weight-lifters might suggest the exercises are designed for mesomorphs, the body type which puts on muscle almost effortlessly, like Mark's. Throughout the demonstration, he uses light weights and very high repetitions, up to fifteen reps per set! This is a regimen for fat people who want to trim down or "easy gainers" like mesomorph Mark. A thin person—or hard gainer—would be advised to look elsewhere and do heavy weights and low reps, standard advice every personal trainer knows. But the implicit message of the video seems to be, Hey, if it works for Mark, it will work for you.

The most interesting autobiographical revelations of the workout video occur in the concluding ten-minute segment on nutrition. It begins with an obese member of his entourage, Kizzy, feeding at a trough of forbidden pleasures: pancakes, hero sandwiches, pizza.

Mark scolds, "Kizzy! You pig! What are you doing?"

Kizzy says, "Eatin' some grub."

Mark turns to Gold's in-house nutritionist, Neal Spruce. Wahlberg grills him for nutrition tips with surprising intensity. During the workout, Mark is completely in charge. During the nutrition portion, he becomes a humble student. His intense interest in the diet tips when he grills the expert, Spruce, adds weight to speculation that Wahlberg may be a binge eater. He has implied as much in interviews.

His weight does fluctuate noticeably. When he stopped smoking in the early 1990s, he was horrified by the disfiguring weight gain. "When I quit smoking, I started eating like a pig," he said the year before he made the workout video. "So I joined a gym, right down the street from my house, and started to work out. It was really painful at first, but once I got over the initial difficulty of changing my lifestyle—I changed my eating habits, too—I found I could really put my whole self into working out at the gym."

Friends say Wahlberg has since resumed smoking, which may explain why he appears winded in the video.

Spruce rejects the current fad of high protein, low carbohydrates, and only enough fat to avoid anorexia! In line with professional nutritionists, instead of best-selling fad diet books, Spruce endorses carbohydrates as energy to fuel Mark's workout.

Other tips which are printed on the screen as Spruce or Mark describes them include (1) eat four complete meals a day; (2) never miss a meal or, if you do, replace it with a carbohydrate drink or fruit bar; and (3) eat your largest meal two hours before you train.

Wisely, Mark urges viewers to incorporate aerobic exercise (aka "cardio") such as the stair climber, treadmill, or stationary bike. "Diet alone won't lose fat," he says. Ironically, there are no aerobic exercises in the video. Obviously Mark doesn't need to lose fat since he appears to have close to zero-percent body fat. On another occasion, Mark explained why aerobics didn't make his video. He doesn't bike or tread. "When I can, I work out every day. But I don't do aerobics. I get that onstage."

At the end of the video, Mark jumps into a Jacuzzi with six bikini-clad women. He disappears under the bubbles, leaving the rest to the viewer's imagination as the credits roll.

While the tape lasts only seventy minutes and pushes light weights, Mark's real-life routine, which he described a few years before the video, is a bit different—and considerably longer. "I lift weights every day for an hour and a half. I do free weights and lots of dumbbells for shaping and size." In the video, he mostly sticks to Smith machines rather than "free weights" (i.e., barbells and dumbbells). "The heaviest weight I've lifted is about three hundred pounds. Every other day, I work on my chest and triceps. Other days, I'll do my back and biceps, then my legs and shoulders. My legs are the weakest part, but I'm working on them!"

That may be why he rarely exposes them on the video.

The tape suggests working all body parts every time you train. Mark's description of his real routine outside the soundstage or mansion living room is more effective. He alternates body parts, giving each a twenty-four-hour rest so the muscles can rebuild before being stressed again. Most busy people, however, can't hit the gym every day and alternate body parts, so his video may have been designed for couch potatoes to get them off the couch and into the gym.

The video certainly got people into stores. VideoScan, which charts consumer sales, reports the tape sold 21,000 units—a muscular showing, if not quite in the slash-and-burn terrain of video workout maven Jane Fonda or even Richard Simmons, but enough to ensure his Mercedes would never run out of gas.

And clearly his routine works. Mark quickly dropped the thirty pounds he gained after quitting cigarettes and described his measurements with pride in 1992. "My arms are about sixteen and a quarter inches. I have a thirty-one-inch waist, and sixteen-and-a-quarter-inch biceps," he added redundantly. "I'm not too sure about my chest, but it's beginning to look good. I don't wanna be so big that I can't move around. I just wanna stay fit," he said with understatement.

Before talking to nutritionist Spruce, Mark pushed protein, not carbs. "Along with working out, I try to eat a lot of protein, like chicken. And I avoid fatty food. When I gave up smoking, I used to stuff the food in my mouth to replace the cigarettes. Now, I eat real well. I'll never go back to cigarettes and food binges." At twenty-one, Wahlberg was already self-conscious enough about his appearance and eating habits to use a term most often employed by serious overeaters—"bingeing."

His precocious musculature, rare for someone his age, when most young men are still thin and desperate to muscle up, has led some to wonder if his physique has been, uh, chemically enhanced. In more than one interview, Mark has vehemently denied taking steroids. That was on the record. But even when he wasn't talking for attribution, Wahlberg could be a Nazi when it came to the mere mention of steroids. When a good friend brought the subject up, Wahlberg gave him a stern lecture, then offered a muscle-gaining tip that never made it into the video or a magazine interview.

Apparently, the guys at his penthouse were sitting around and someone mentioned steroids. Mark interrupted angrily. "What are you talking about? You don't need that shit," he said to one of his trainers. "What the fuck are you doing?"

Then he offered this tip to stimulate the appetite for a "natural" weight gain: "Just eat," he told his trainer, "and smoke a little dope. . . ."

In 1993, the same year he was obsessing about weight gain and body image, something made Mark Wahlberg even more self-conscious, and it had nothing to do with his body. He already had the brawn, as the home workout video brilliantly shows. Brains were another matter. Rich beyond his wildest fantasies in the old Dorchester days, Mark still felt insecure about his lack of formal education. Actually, the term he used was "ashamed."

So just as he tackled the battle of the bulge with a workout routine from hell, he attacked his lack of a high-school diploma with the same intensity. Unfortunately, it seemed easier for him to develop six-pack abs than to pass the GED.

Only twenty-one, he knew he was a role model and had publicly condemned the violence of rap and the glamorization of drugs and booze. He even quit cigarettes so kids wouldn't think it was cool to light up. He also didn't want teenagers to follow in his academic footsteps.

Sadly he said, "I'm twenty-one, and I'm a high-school dropout." But he was working on fixing that problem. "I've learned a lot in the past year, but school is still a priority for me, and that's why I'm going back to get my GED. I got all my tests done except science. Science, boy, I'm terrified of science, but I *will* pass, because I want it, and I'll work hard for it, you know what I'm saying? I'm gonna have my diploma. Then, when I need to learn more about business and the real world, I can go and take a course. It's like I feel almost *ashamed* about being a dropout and not being able to go to my prom and graduate with my class," he said in an interview with Debi Cohen in the February 1993 issue of *YM* magazine.

On another occasion, the rapper offered a more practical reason for the importance of a formal education. Being "book-smart" would make him even more street-smart. A framed diploma on the wall might look nice and make him a better role model for would-be dropouts, but what he could do with that diploma also motivated him to study for the GED. "You can motherfuckin' snake and connive any shit you want in life if you got education. Then you know how to use that shit to your advantage and trick motherfuckers and shit. You be the man."

Sometimes it seemed Mark was his own worst critic. During long bus trips between gigs, he could be found in the back of the luxury van, curled up with a science textbook and beating himself up for not passing the GED. "Science is the worst, man. Sometimes when I'm stuck on the bus studying a science book, I say, 'I could have had this done three years ago if I wasn't such a lazy hardhead.' You know what I'm sayin'?" he told Jon Pareles in the April 8, 1992, issue of the *New York Times*. (In 1991, Wahlberg had taken and passed four of the six tests for the GED. That same year, a lapsed Catholic, he returned to the Church and was finally confirmed at the ripe old age of twenty.)

In 1994, Mark was still studying for the GED, but the science portion of the test continued to thwart him. Today the GED; tomorrow, the world of college. Although "tomorrow" never came, Mark said he planned on going to college once he earned his high-school equivalency diploma.

While Mark studied for the exams, he didn't have time to worry about more commercial considerations, like an accent that at times is almost unintelligible on the workout video. His speaking voice during the on-camera workout reflects his Boston roots. He also uses double negatives and other classic examples of bad grammar. The video makes a nice time capsule, showing a young man still under construction, not only physically, but vocally.

In less than two years, Mark would ditch his blue-collar accent in *Fear* and play a sophisticated charmer who also happens to be a psycho. In interviews with the *New York Times* and *Newsweek*, his grammar and usage became impeccable. Just as he worked on his body, he apparently pumped up with a vocal coach and grammarian. A man who could figure out how to develop enormous sixteen-inch "guns," as bodybuilders affectionately/psychotically label their biceps, could certainly find a way to harden his *r*'s and soften a harsh Boston brogue. He would learn to park his Jeep Cherokee in the "Harvard Yard," not the "Hah-vuhd Yahd."

In 1993, the year the workout video came out, the public couldn't get enough of Mark's body. *Playgirl* put him on the cover of its May issue, while inside it zoomed in for a close-up of his third nipple, about two inches below the left one. The editors helpfully drew a big circle around the thing, which actually looks like a birthmark. The publication also quoted Mark on the anatomical aberration, which he didn't consider a defect, but rather the male equivalent of the mythical G-spot. "It's cool. It's unique. Not too many people have them, and it's not hazardous to my health or anything. It's not something to be ashamed about. It's dope [translation from the original rap: *for real*]. And bitches like to suck it." Strangely, and mistakenly, the magazine also claimed he was only five-feet-four inches tall!

Mark's appearance on the cover of *Playgirl* made sense: the magazine is targeted at women, but rumors claim *Playgirl*'s own fiercely guarded marketing surveys show its readership is largely gay.

No one ever made that claim about *Penthouse*, a gynecological guide to the female form, but two months before Mark appeared in *Playgirl*, *Penthouse* put him on the cover of its March issue—shirtless, as usual. To ensure that grossed-out heterosexual men wouldn't run fleeing from newsstands, Natalie, *Penthouse*'s "Pet of the Month," also posed on the cover and inside.

The photo spread's "body language" spoke volumes. While Natalie has her hands all over Mark's body, he barely touches her. His crotch, which he grabs in several photos, gets more hands-on attention than the poor *Penthouse* Pet.

So what was a muscle boy doing on the cover of a magazine designed for heavy-breathing heterosexuals? *Penthouse*'s senior editor, Peter Bloch, blamed it on an unlikely coalition . . . the Moral Majority, and what the Majority might call feminazis.

At the time, Bloch told me, newsstand vendors were "taking severe hits from feminists and the Moral Majority." Dealers promised *Penthouse* it would get better rack placement with "covers that were very sanitary." Vendors felt putting a guy and a gal on the cover would somehow "sanitize" *Penthouse*'s notorious lesbian erotica. The experiment lasted about a year "and bombed, circulation-wise," Bloch said.

For a guy to land on its cover, *Penthouse* required two things: a hot career—no surprise—but also good verbal skills. Wahlberg obviously fulfilled the first requirement. Bloch said, "He was all over every billboard in Manhattan." But even more impressively, the editor told me Mark's interview had been so interesting, it cinched the cover.

The same year the video came out, Mark briefly dated actress Shannen Doherty. If Mark had a bad-boy image at the time, Doherty's was "worst girl." Her behavior even warranted an entire newsletter devoted to it, entitled, *I Hate Brenda*, named for her character on *Beverly Hills, 90210*. Her behavior seemed contagious. *People* magazine ran a photo of the couple in a tender moment at the Brat Pack's home away from home, the Roxbury, on the Sunset Strip, right across from his defaced billboard. Mark and Shannen are flipping the photographer the bird.

CHAPTER 11

Career ER (Emergency Resuscitation)

If 1993 was a nightmare of bad behavior and worse publicity, after alleged gay- and Madonna-bashings, 1994 was a dream come true for Mark's career, which had been floundering even before the retaliation by activists and Madonna's overcaffeinated record exec. Less than a year after its release, his second CD, *You Gotta Believe*, had hit the remainder bins and his career had hit the skids. Marky Mark's next public appearance might have been on late-night infomercials, plugging the Amazing Incredible Combination Abdominal Tummy Tucker/Weed Whacker, with Mark as spokes-stud. Or a Golden Oldies nostalgia tour with L. L. Kool J and MC Hammer sometime in the next millennium.

Then a funny thing happened. A-list director Penny Marshall saw one of his lively rap videos and put Mark Wahlberg on her "to-do" list of must-audition actors for *Renaissance Man*. She also had noticed the heavy breathing by both women and men at a Calvin Klein fashion show as Mark strutted the runway. "I saw the reaction to him and said, 'Bring that kid in,'" Marshall recalled of her ringside sighting in the May 1998 issue of *Premiere* magazine. As in the case of *The Substitute*, Wahlberg came to the acting audition for his big break less than prepared. He hadn't read the script this time, either. He only agreed to meet with Marshall and the film's star, Danny DeVito, because he was a fan of theirs, not of filmmaking.

"I just wanted to meet Penny Marshall and Danny DeVito—I grew up in love with those two—*I didn't want to be in the movie*," he said.

Penny Marshall, a role model during his formative years?! That's not as preposterous as it sounds. Mark grew up blue-collar and fond of beer. Marshall's sitcom character, Shirley's pal Laverne, shared the same roots and manufactured a product he loved.

So, even though Wahlberg didn't like movies, he *loved* 1970s sitcoms, and Wahlberg came to the back lot at Disney that pivotal day, not to read for *Renaissance Man*, but to meet his teen idol, Laverne DeFazio, as he later told *Interview* magazine in October 1997.

Marshall turned her groupie into a collaborator. "By the time I walked out of the meeting, I wanted to try to be in their movie. Then I read the script [!], which I should have done beforehand," Mark told Stephen Rebello in the June 1997 issue of *Movieline* magazine.

Wahlberg's chiseled body at the Calvin Klein fashion klatch caught Marshall's attention first, but it was his street accent that held it. After auditioning one too many Yale drama school grads faking street-tough, Marshall knew the real thing when she heard it. "Danny DeVito and I had been looking desperately for a kid who sounds like us," said the Brooklyn-born director, who, unlike her young star, has never bothered to lose an accent that has permanently typecast her geographically.

"Julliard knocks it out of them. But Mark read and he said 'ambalence.' 'An ambalence came down the block.' He talked the way we do," Marshall said in the May 1998 issue of *Premiere* magazine.

When she asked the rapper if he had read the script, a strange question in the middle of an audition, Mark lied to his idol. "Yeah, of course I read the script," he told her. Later he confessed, "I was acting like I was interested, because I just wanted to meet them."

So how did Laverne convert gangsta Marky Mark into Mark Wahlberg, serious actuh? It was her 'tude, dude!—as his generation likes to say. "I was there with them, and I could tell they really thought I could do it. Me. Not Marky Mark. That faith was everything. . . . I just remember it being so different from any other meeting that I'd had with directors or producers or studio people or whatever. For the first time, someone said, 'If you want to do this, we think you could play this part. Would you be interested in trying to show us that you can do it?' By that time I was just so in love with them that I said, 'Yeah, I'll do anything.'" (All this Mark told *Interview* magazine for its October 1997 issue.)

Wahlberg's willingness to cooperate with the filmmakers even extended to reading a 120-page screenplay. However, at heart he still had some reluctance about becoming a movie star. "When I was making music, there were already some preconceived notions, and people were saying this and that about me, and so I was just going out of my way to be real out there. The last thing I wanted to do was act."

There's a genuine repugnance in the music world toward the movie world. Punk rockers, and even more so grunge artists, consider signing on for a Hollywood movie selling out. Courtney Love almost passed on her career-making role in *The People vs. Larry Flynt* (1996) because her grungy peers gave her so much grief. Wahlberg had an even grungier image as a gangsta to uphold.

"I had worked with Scott Kalvert on many occasions. He did my music videos, and he was always telling me how I could be in the movies. But I was like, whatever, you know, save that acting stuff for all them Hollywood *punks*. I was shooting videos and making rap records. It wasn't that long since I'd gotten out of prison." Even stranger than Mark's reference to doing hard time is his time frame. It wasn't "that long" since he'd gotten out of prison? *Renaissance Man* came out in 1994. He'd been incarcerated a good six years earlier. Maybe the experience had been so traumatic it was still fresh in his memory, though more than half a decade old.

Still traumatized, perhaps—but not so numb that Mark couldn't feel a happier emotion: gratitude for the maker of his new career. "I literally owe Penny everything and I love her. She deserves some major butt-smooching," he gushed. "*Renaissance Man* gave me the acting bug."

An authority no less prestigious than the *New York Times Magazine* approved of Mark's decision: "Wahlberg chose his movie projects carefully, starting out small and declining to capitalize on his image as a hunk," it said in a major piece, the length usually accorded world figures like Gorbachev or Gretzsky.

Instead of going the usual route, a starring role in a vanity production with an independent film company, Wahlberg took a small role in a big studio movie, content to fade into the background as part of an ensemble cast. Too many hot TV stars don't have the savvy or humility that tyro Wahlberg displayed, and they end up with Luke Perry's feature-film résumé.

Renaissance Man was a high-concept film. In the movie industry, "high concept" means you can summarize the plot in one simple, declarative sentence. A good example: "Shark terrorizes resort community" *(Jaws)*. Bad example: "Obsessive-compulsive narcissistic novelist becomes a better man after falling in love with a codependent waitress and his gay neighbor's adorable dog" *(As Good As It Gets)*. And best example: "Really big ship sinks" *(Titanic)*.

The high concept of *Renaissance Man* was probably pitched to studio executives with a simple sentence like this: "*Dead Poets Society* meets *Stripes*." Or since the cultural references of thirty-something development executives at movie studios are 1970s sitcoms, the pitch may have been "*Welcome Back, Kotter* in camouflage pants."

Instead of the Ivy League preppies Robin Williams taught in *Dead Poets*, the characters in *Renaissance Man* were the ones who probably took shop in high school. The ensemble consists of eight army recruits who are so stupid they are in danger of being mustered out of basic training. The smarter GIs call them "the Double D's," short for "dumb as dogshit."

An unemployed ad executive (Danny DeVito) reluctantly signs on to teach these G.I. Joes and one G.I. Jane. In his big-screen debut, Mark plays one of the Double D's, Tommy Lee Haywood, from Willocoochee, Georgia. He's a bad ole boy from the backwoods who joined the army for a view of the world wider than the one available from the window of his trailer-park home, as he says in the film. Mark's character is a brawler, almost a thug, and the role made him leery of being typecast. But his affection for Penny Marshall and Danny DeVito compelled him to take the job anyway.

"In the path that I was on, I was destined to be typecast [as] the asshole, you know? The tough guy who probably gets the girl for a minute, then gets beat up or dies. Which is cool—it's a part I love to watch—but I don't want to be restricted to just playing that," he said three years later, to Peter McQuaid for the October 1997 *Out* magazine after a kaleidoscope of roles proved that Mark truly had avoided typecasting.

Wahlberg felt *Renaissance Man*'s G.I. brawler reinforced the stereotype, although his part in the ensemble was so tiny—in fact, the smallest of the group—that his character wasn't even allowed to fall in love or die, just punch out a black soldier a couple of times in a weirdly autobiographical hint of his pursuit of black schoolgirls years earlier.

Renaissance Man is a strange movie to watch on video. Marketed as a comedy, it's actually a character study with a few lame punch lines. When DeVito asks his students if they've heard of Shakespeare, all but one is clueless, and even he's on shaky ground when he responds to DeVito, "Isn't that the guy who hangs out in Central Park every summer?" Ditto the identity of Hamlet: "That's about a little bitty pig, right?"

The film never found an audience, which seemed to be people who like unfunny farces. *Renaissance Man* grossed only $24 million at the box office in the United States and Canada. The reviews were contemptuous. Janet Maslin of the *New York Times* dissed the movie but loved its hip-hopping G.I.s: "*Renaissance Man* runs longer than two hours and would have been funnier with some of its padding removed. Yet even at its present length, the film has some confusing lapses. . . . *Renaissance Man* does succeed in assembling a highly likable band of recruits. The actors are appealing. . . ." Wahlberg must have been glad he liked Marshall's Laverne enough to overcome his fear of filming when he read: "Mark Wahlberg, playing a tough Southern soldier who finds ample reasons to take his shirt off, oozes gritty confidence and makes a strong, swaggering impression on the big screen." You can be sure Alma Wahlberg filed that *New York Times* review in the same archives that house her son's underwear photos.

Not only does Wahlberg take his shirt off in *Renaissance Man*, he gets a semi-nude shower scene inserted for no apparent reason other than to showcase skin and prove his admission that he can't sing in real life. His rendition of "Achy Breaky Heart" while sudsing up, makes the viewer's ears feel the same way as his heart. The shower scene is more saddening than erotic, however. Mark was already feeling like a piece of meat, "the exploitation of Marky Mark," as he put it, when Marshall decided to zoom in on his chest. He could console himself with a well-praised screen debut and a knack for accents. Wahlberg managed to ditch his Boston brogue and fake a cracker drawl.

His desire to dump his rapper image on-screen while still selling records is evident in *Renaissance Man*. The end credits reveal that he wrote and/or performed four songs for the soundtrack, but he never raps on-screen. You can hear him rapping off-screen, but when it comes time for the Double D's to perform a hip-hop riff on *Hamlet* in class, Mark doesn't participate. While his fellow Shakespearean scholars perform the elaborately choreographed "Hamlet Rap," Wahlberg remains seated at his desk and plays "air bongos" on his schoolroom desk.

It's even more ironic that he co-wrote the music and lyrics, which reveal a sophisticated familiarity with the play, something his dimbulb character doesn't have. In fact, his only embarrassing moment on-screen, except possibly the one under the shower tap, has him describing Laertes' motivation in *Hamlet* using double negatives and lots of "ain't"s.

As a major rap star with a platinum album and two platinum singles gilding his résumé, Wahlberg was subjected to enormous pressure by Disney, which bankrolled the production, to lend his fame and name to the film and do an on-screen set. The fact that he didn't suggests why he has his current film career, and another rapper-turned-movie star, MC Hammer, has his. Don't play yourself on-screen if you want to be a Hollywood player.

Renaissance Man was only Mark's first feature film, but he had the self-possession to butt heads with Jeffrey Katzenberg, Disney's production chief, notorious as a micro-manager who managed himself out of the number two job at the "not-so-happiest place on earth." Wahlberg recalled to Dale Brasel in the May 1997 issue of *Detour* magazine, "You don't know the fights I had over that shit. . . . For any other actor it would be okay [to perform his music], but at that early stage, if anything like that was recognizable, it would just throw the rest of the movie out of the window. And I didn't want to fuck up anybody's movie. What am I most famous for, you know?"

Unlike Katzenberg, Penny Marshall didn't exert any demands on the actor to rap on-camera. In fact, she considered his behavior generous rather than temperamental. Perhaps unaware that he was desperately trying to shed his hip-hop image, she thought he surrendered the dance floor to his costars out of humility and egolessness, not because of career calculations. "Mark wrote a great rap for the film. Then he had to put his own ego aside and teach the other actors to do it, because his character would never rap," she said, referring to the fact that Mark's good ole boy from Willocoochee would more likely do a hoedown than hip-hop. "He was very generous about it."

Wahlberg's rejection of his rapper roots represented more than a good career move. It was his desire to be taken seriously as an actor, not a gangsta who shoves his hands down his pants onstage. He was by now also repelled by what rap had become. Never a pretty picture, the whole hip-hop scene had turned downright ugly in Mark's mind. While his "manager self" distanced himself from the music for career purposes, his "moral self" ran screaming from "artists" who hated women and urged listeners to kill cops.

"Marky Mark was made into something false and became a character these record-company people were selling randomly," he said to a national publication. But the commercialization of Marky Mark was not the most compelling reason he fled the stage and recording studio in the mid-1990s. "The whole rap world is at a really negative place now, convincing Middle America that these guys are out killing people and admitting it on records. I don't take what they say seriously, but other people obviously do. I listen to Tupac [Shakur], mesmerized by the way he wrote his own fate, in a way. When he got shot, it seemed so fake and scripted, like, 'Okay, this is the ultimate marketing scheme.' When he died, I was devastated."

And maybe more than a little bit afraid for his own life if he continued in an art form where people literally "died for their art."

Marky Mark and the Funky Bunch (1990). (PHOTO BY ANN BOGART)

The hot young singing attraction in 1990. (PHOTO BY ANN BOGART)

Marky Mark smiling for his fans in 1992. (PHOTO BY ANN BOGART)

Doing his trademark routine, dropping trousers for a crowd at a Los Angeles basketball game.
(PHOTO BY B. KING/GAMMA LIAISON)

In a feisty moment. (PHOTO BY W. STAMBLER/SYGMA)

Mark and his brother Donnie. (PHOTO COURTESY OF CORBIS/LYNN GOLDSMITH)

Mark with Leonardo DiCaprio, his costar in *The Basketball Diaries* (1995). (PHOTO COURTESY OF CORBIS/LYNN GOLDSMITH)

Mark Wahlberg and Burt Reynolds in a scene from *Boogie Nights* (1997).
(PHOTO COURTESY OF GAMMA LIAISON)

he serious actor in the late 1990s.
HOTO COURTESY OF GAMMA LIAISON/GILLES DECAMPS/PULP IMAGE)

Presenters Mark Wahlberg and Jennifer Lopez at the MTV Video Music Awards in September 1998. (PHOTO COURTESY OF AP PHOTO/MICHAEL CAULFIELD)

CHAPTER 12

White Shoes Diary

Penny Marshall may have infected the reluctant movie star with the "acting bug," but his next film made him positively feverish about continuing his movie career. Scott Kalvert, the director of his music videos, had long encouraged the photogenic rapper to make the transition to the big screen. But it wasn't until he showed him the script for *The Basketball Diaries* (1995), Kalvert's first feature, that Wahlberg abandoned his "I'm a rapper, not an actor" riff. And this time, he actually read the screenplay *before* the audition.

"I wanted it immediately, as soon as I read the script. Before I even finished it. I knew I could do it and bring some of my own feelings and experiences to it," Mark said. Kalvert wanted Wahlberg, too, but the production company, Island, and its distributor, New Line Cinema, needed to be convinced. The official press kit from New Line chirpily says, "After an impressive cold reading, Wahlberg landed the role." Not exactly. In fact, insiders say the cautious studio made the novice jump through . . . well, the acting equivalent of basketball hoops—six nerve-wracking auditions.

The screenplay was based on the cult classic, *The Basketball Diaries*, poet Jim Carroll's autobiographical novel about growing up poor, thuggish, and drug-addicted in New York during the mid-1960s. The book had a classy pedigree, first serialized in *The Paris Review*, a highbrow literary journal, in 1968, before publication in book form a decade later.

Because it was a cult novel, *The Basketball Diaries* attracted a huge following of actors and directors who wanted to bring Carroll's elliptical prose and nightmarish scenarios to the big screen. The film was about to go into production at Columbia Pictures back in 1988, when Coca-Cola bought the studio. A graphic movie about heroin use was not the kind of image sought by a company whose slogan was "Things go better with . . ." Humorous allusions to what kind of "coke" the manufacturer was talking about were already making the rounds when the film was announced. Coke's execs read *The Basketball Diaries* script and passed on the project.

Years later, when the movie finally went into production and he had a bit role in the film as a junkie poet, author Carroll described the conservative mind-set of the studios in the 1980s when the project first made the Hollywood rounds. During a break in shooting, Carroll recalled for Claudia Eller of the *Los Angeles Times* (January 25, 1995): "In the Reagan years, the studios were really gun-shy about this. It took a long time for the movie to get made. Everything has its time."

By 1995, times had definitely changed. The *Reefer Madness* mentality of the Reagan era had long since vanished. Heroin chic and its spokesmodels, anorexic teen models like Kate Moss and Milla Jovovich, had advertisers just saying yes, to the image if not the reality of drug use. If junkie chic could sell everything from perfume to Victoria's Secret, it could probably fill movie theaters, too. The project finally got a green light from Island Pictures, whose distributor is the Tiffany's of independents, New Line Cinema. Scott Kalvert signed on to direct. Although he was only thirty years old with no feature-film credits, his videos for Will Smith, Cyndi Lauper, and, of course, Marky Mark, had caught the attention of Island and New Line. The MTV generation was the exact demographic studios wanted in theaters since the eighteen- to twenty-five-year-old crowd, besides having lots of disposable income, also tends to see a movie it likes more than once, the only way a film has a shot at cracking the $100 million blockbuster barrier.

New Line and Island's decision to hire Kalvert, a music-video veteran but novice filmmaker, had a precedent, however discouraging. *Alien³*, with its $70 million budget, was handed over to a twenty-six-year-old video director, David Fincher, whose most famous credit was an Orwellian *1984*-ish TV commercial for IBM. The third *Alien* picture was a major disaster artistically and financially when it came out in 1992, but three years later the lesson was apparently forgotten when New Line decided to give a barely thirty-something novice a chance. But the studio hedged its bets, insisting on setting the movie in the present, to save expenses on costumes, cars, and locations. Plus Kalvert had a preposterously tiny budget, $4 million, to realize his vision.

Besides saving money on expensive period trappings, *The Basketball Diaries*' modern-day setting allowed the use of contemporary pop songs. The soundtrack CD could be released and turned into multiple music videos. The production company's hot record label, Island Alive, did just that, and a spin-off video from the film enjoyed daily rotation on MTV, better promotion than a paid TV commercial . . . and it was free!

Every young actor begged for a role, either as the lead or even in a supporting role, because the script, by Bryan Goluboff, twenty-seven, was so well written. Among the unlikely suitors for parts in the project over the years were Matt Dillon, a bit long in the tooth to play a high-school basketball player; Eric Stoltz (same age problem); and Anthony Michael Hall, who seemed on permanent career hiatus at the time, but had been the original star planned for the 1989 project until real-life problems made the film seem a bit too autobiographical. Among the more realistic candidates were Ethan Hawke (a real contender after *Dead Poets Society*) and River Phoenix, the hottest actor of his generation and the only one with an Oscar nomination (*Running on Empty,* 1988) under his belt. In fact, the day Phoenix received news of his Oscar nod, MTV asked him what he wanted to do next. Instead of responding, "I'm going to Disneyland," Phoenix pulled out a battered copy of *The Basketball Diaries* and said, "I want to play Jim Carroll." The sad irony is that in some cosmic way, Phoenix, who died of a drug overdose in 1993, *did* play Carroll, without the author's redemptive ending.

It wasn't completely surprising that Leonardo DiCaprio eventually beat out all these worthies for the lead of Jim, a star basketball player who starts out sniffing glue and ends up chasing a drug dealer off a six-story-high building. DiCaprio had already made a huge impression in one of his early screen roles, *What's Eating Gilbert Grape?* (1993), as a sweetly retarded youth who likes to hang out atop telephone poles. The literally wordless role earned Leonardo an Oscar nomination.

But what was really surprising was that with only one feature-film credit and a frivolous image as a poster boy, Wahlberg made the onscreen basketball team. It was his good fortune that Kalvert believed in him enough, based on their video collaborations, to ignore the public image and see the talented actor underneath the 100-percent-cotton underwear and abs of steel. Kalvert's faith in his video star would be rewarded with an accomplished performance by an embryonic movie star. Ironically, more than one critic would wryly note that Wahlberg's work was superior to his mentor/discoverer's contributions as director.

When Wahlberg said he could bring "some of my own experiences and feelings" to the film, and "I could play [this] part in my sleep," it was an understatement and not immodesty. The character of Mickey in *The Basketball Diaries* had many elements that were similar to his own life.

Wahlberg may not have been too happy, though, when he read screenwriter Goluboff's description of Mickey: "He has badness in him." In contrast, DiCaprio's "character was always ambivalent toward violence." The main key to all the characters, Goluboff said, was "their relationship to evil," and Mickey was its living embodiment. *The Basketball Diaries* is a slice-of-life movie, dissected with a machete. The New York streets DiCaprio, Wahlberg, and their fellow basketball players roam are beyond mean. There's a sixteen-year-old hooker, played by an uncredited Juliette Lewis, who is so strung out on heroin her services are available for $15, with the price constantly dropping in tandem with the amount of smack in her bloodstream. There's the basketball coach (Bruno Kirby), the only nurturing teacher at the team's brutal parochial school, who turns out be nurturing for all the wrong reasons. He's a pedophile who offers the star of the team money for sex—in the shower.

Basketball provides an escape from this life in Hell's Kitchen (that section on the West Side of midtown Manhattan made famous by so many gangster films of the 1940s and 1950s). In the opening voice-over, DiCaprio says: "We were the hottest high-school basketball team in New York City. We felt like nothing could stop us." The death from leukemia of a fellow player, the best on the team, does stop them, however, and they begin their descent, from sniffing solvent to mainlining smack. The team's hoop dreams become a nightmare when they mistakenly ingest downers instead of uppers just before the big game. Their incompetent choice of drugs sounds funny, like something from a Cheech and Chong movie or the 1930s camp documentary, *Reefer Madness,* but Kalvert directs it as tragedy, not farce.

Kicked off the team and out of school, the four teens turn to increasingly vicious forms of street crime. Stealing jewelry out of classmates' lockers escalates to robbing candy stores, boosting cars, and violently mugging little old ladies. The team members hit bottom after pushing a drug dealer, who sold them ersatz heroin for $35, off the roof of a building to his death. DiCaprio's Jim escapes; Wahlberg's Mickey, who pushed the guy, gets a ten- to fifteen-year sentence after being tried as an adult.

Making the movie was an exorcism for Mark, and it must have been painful, since some of the scenes came close to autobiography, often paralleling "my own feelings and experiences," as he said. The muggings were probably the most uncomfortable to re-create for Mark. After knocking down a helpful senior citizen who stops to give him directions, Wahlberg's Mickey steals her purse and then proceeds to kick her violently.

You get the feeling the scene hurt Wahlberg psychically more than it damaged the well-trained stuntwoman who knew how to take a blow, even though she looked like everybody's grandmother. As Mark told Jeanne Wolf of the *New York Daily News* (April 16, 1995): "It's really tough to have to do that stuff, because you're not working with people you dislike. I had to rob an older woman in the film and rough her up. Even though she was a stuntwoman, it still wasn't very gentlemanly."

At this point in his life and growing maturity, "gentleman" was the term often used to describe the courtly young actor from the mean streets of Boston. Other scenes of violence in *The Basketball Diaries* also held autobiographical resonance and must have seemed like flashbacks to Mark. In the film, Wahlberg's Mickey smashes a beer bottle in the face of a basketball player from an opposing team, then kicks him while he's down. The beer-bottle incident is particularly eerie since it was the theft of a beer and a mugging that had led to Wahlberg's prison sentence eight years earlier. You wonder if he felt renewed remorse shooting take after take of the fictional assaults.

In a less painful bit of screen autobiography, Wahlberg's movie alter-ego beats up a friend who shouts out the generic insult, "Fuck your mother!" Wahlberg adores his mom, as more than one friend has told me. So you suspect he didn't have to do much acting when he screams at his buddy, "Don't you ever say that about my mother!" then bitch-slaps him, to use Quentin Tarantino's phrase.

At least one part of *The Basketball Diaries* was non-autobiographical for Mark. In real life, Mark has a wonderful, supportive brother, Donnie. In the film, however, Mark's older brother fences stolen autos. When Mark fails to deliver a promised Lincoln Towncar, his brother breaks his arm in a scene that is painful to watch.

The pivotal element of the movie, drug use, was also not autobiographical, according to Mark in a national magazine interview, although his equivocal use of the phrase "compared to . . ." leaves room for doubt. On the set, Wahlberg said, "Compared to this guy, I'm so clean, man, it's ridiculous. I swear—and I wouldn't just say this for an interview—but I don't do any of those drugs. It's just acting for me. People said, 'Why don't you try it [drugs] for the movie?' and that's just so lame, you know? You do drugs like that and it gives you an excuse to do them again."

As painful as the re-creations of his life may have been, the film also must have been a relief because it suggests a way his real life could have evolved if it hadn't been turned around by prison and his personal angel, Emily. Wahlberg said about Mickey, "He's the type of person who feels that if he can overpower somebody physically, it's safe to hang out with them. [DiCaprio's] Jim, who is very strong psychologically, keeps Mickey in check, until he gets too far out there. Then no one can stop him. Mickey had a real chance to make a career out of his physical abilities, but never got the encouragement or direction to do it. There is nothing around him to give him the slightest belief that he can make something of himself, so he doesn't really try," Mark said. Like Mickey, Marky had a chance to make a career out of his "physical abilities" in concert and on billboards. Unlike Mickey, a strong support group made Mark believe in himself enough to become a major movie star. This is, after all, the same self-possessed young man who once said, "Anything I put my mind to I can accomplish."

Another element of the film didn't bother Wahlberg one bit. Despite his own run-ins with substances licit and illicit, he felt that *The Basketball Diaries* did anything but glorify drug use. While Madison Avenue coined the term "heroin chic," the film embodied what might have been called "heroin grotesque." In fact, Wahlberg believed the story served as a public-service announcement of sorts, although much more sophisticated than "Just say no!" sloganeering or sunny-side-up eggs symbolizing brains fried from drugs. "The raw and honest depiction of the drug scenes," Mark informed a national journal, "would help demystify heroin, cocaine, and other drugs and perhaps discourage people from doing them." To make the depiction genuinely raw, the stars found themselves taking lessons from a peer group counselor for an arms-on learning experience that stopped just short of sticking the needle into a vein. "We shot in New York, where all this stuff really happened. We learned from a drug counselor how to shoot heroin—not that we did. We just prepared for the movie. That film was intense," Mark said.

The Basketball Diaries is clearly DiCaprio's show, and it would be hype to say Wahlberg steals it. However, the novice manages to make magnificent petty thefts whenever he shares the screen with the lead. And while DiCaprio has a multidimensional character to work with, a street thug with the soul of a poet and the collapsed veins of a smackhead, Wahlberg is stuck playing an unredeemable jerk who cracks jokes after the funeral of a friend.

Director Kalvert cannily continued the fleshploitation of Marky Mark in ways that even a compulsive exhibitionist might have found invasive. In one scene, the basketball coach (Kirby), a child molester who likes teens, opens the doors of bathroom stalls, allegedly looking for cigarette smokers, but he's really just on a voyeuristic trip. Behind one door there's Mark, sitting on the toilet and snarling, "Hey, I'm taking a dump here!"

More gratuitous nudity pops up. During a tearful wake on a basketball court, mourning the death of their teammate from leukemia, the teenagers decide to play ball in memoriam. It turns into a skins vs. shirts match, except they all remove their shirts! The motivation for the striptease is inexplicable. It's a cold night, and they're shooting baskets in torrential rain.

Endless hours in the rain were just part of the dues Wahlberg and his costars paid while making *The Basketball Diaries*. One sequence was scary even to watch and must have been more terrifying to perform on the set. A favorite pastime of the team is standing on a cliff above the Hudson River, mooning the Cruise Line boat as it passes, then jumping 500 feet into the muck, which, DiCaprio's voice-over elegantly says, "every toilet in New York City has flushed shit into." Amazingly, it appears Wahlberg did his own stunt into this flowing toilet, since his face is clearly visible in midshot as he plummets off the cliff and into the Hudson sewer.

Perhaps it was this jump into the muck together that bonded Mark and Leonardo. Whatever made them become best buds who still talk on the phone regularly, Mark and Leonardo did not begin filming as bros. Jealous pros is more like it. DiCaprio felt he was the professional and his costar a lucky amateur who had literally muscled his way into a project for which he was creatively underqualified.

Wahlberg called the film a "hectic experience" that began with "less than perfect" bonding between himself and DiCaprio. Age differences created part of the tension. It was also a matter of pedigree, the Boston slums and the Academy of Motion Pictures Arts and Sciences coming together for the first time, perhaps.

"We both went into [the film] with a chip on our shoulder," explains Mark in the June 1997 issue of *Movieline*. "Being, to a certain extent, from the world Jim Carroll describes in his book gave me the position to say, 'Hold on. Why is *this* guy doing this? He's from Hollywood.' And him being a great actor, with lots of experience, and the star of the movie, he was like, 'Hold on. We don't want this rapper/underwear model fucking up our beautiful art movie from this classic book.' We both got over it and got along well. I've been on movies where there's this fake, 'I love you,' then you see somebody later and they don't even want to look at you. It just wasn't like that here—it was genuine, and it's still like that today."

In fact, their different backgrounds enriched their performances, with each actor providing the other with a glimpse of an unknown world. DiCaprio may, in fact, have been the greater beneficiary, since his "Hollywood" world was farther removed than Wahlberg's Boston from *Diaries*' brutal vision of New York City living.

"It was great working with [DiCaprio] because of the two different worlds we come from. We didn't think we would get along as well as we do. I come from a place where people don't get along with anybody except themselves. But me being from one place and him being from another, we clicked, and we both learned something at the end of the day," Mark told *Movieline* in that mid-1997 interview.

A visitor to the set felt DiCaprio needed a bit of attitude adjustment by his senior, in years if not acting experience. "Wahlberg, twenty-four, has the wary humility of a guy who's been spanked by stardom. DiCaprio, a cocky nineteen, acts like he thinks his star is always going to be on the rise," a reporter from the *Los Angeles Times* wrote.

Wahlberg's "wary humility" was unmerited, another visitor to the set said. "Many people believe he was better in [*The Basketball Diaries*] than DiCaprio," *Movieline* magazine claimed, without identifying its sources.

By the time the gentleman from the *Times* showed up, the one-upmanship had turned into a mutual admiration society. On one occasion, DiCaprio lightheartedly invaded Wahlberg's trailer and his interview. "What's up?" DiCaprio asked in front of a reporter. "You sayin' good things about me?"

"No, whadda ya, kiddin' me?" Wahlberg replied.

"Can I have a cigarette?" DiCaprio asked. Then remembering his day job as role model, Wahlberg said to the reporter, "Oh, hey, I don't smoke."

Both young men, unfortunately, still do—several years and incalculable lung damage later.

DiCaprio wasn't the only person on the set Wahlberg managed to disarm and charm. Despite Mark's thick Boston accent, he developed a dead-on impersonation of former deadhead Jim Carroll, whose Hell's Kitchen accent is inflected with a lisp.

While Wahlberg also charmed reporters on the set, his talents didn't work the same magic on movie critics, who loathed the picture. Happily, some reviewers put down their poison pens long enough to make nice about Mark.

The *Los Angeles Times*' Kenneth Turan wrote, "*The Basketball Diaries* is a lose-lose proposition. Although it masquerades as a cautionary tale about the horrors of heroin, this epic of teenage angst is more accurately seen as a reverential wallow in the gutter of self-absorption. When it's not boring you with its spittle-encrusted delineation of the agonies of addiction, *Basketball Diaries* is romanticizing the ultimate effects of drug use."

One can only wonder if Turan saw the same film everyone else did. Especially powerful was the "romantic" scene where a strung-out, cash-strapped DiCaprio lets a john fellate him in a subway restroom. Far from romanticizing the incident, the movie shows DiCaprio gritting his teeth in pain. In the novel, Carroll "writes lyrically of a blow job he hustles," *Rolling Stone*'s Peter Travers mentioned in his pan of the film, while taking time to also note how "muscled" Mark looks on-screen.

The alternative paper *L.A. Weekly*, which usually loves all things seamy, loathed the picture, which it called unsalvageable despite "the best efforts of DiCaprio and, as one of Jim's sidekicks, Mark Wahlberg." It's interesting that out of the supporting cast, only Wahlberg's performance was singled out for praise.

The usually kind *New York Times'* Janet Maslin was almost as brutal as her Los Angeles counterparts: "As directed by Scott Kalvert with a hollow flashiness that reflects his rock-video background, this story . . . has no special voice or style. This material becomes a roll call of sordid episodes and nasty pranks. The film . . . becomes a series of grim landmarks, supposedly salvaged by the banal idea that Jim will someday make them part of his art." But like the *Los Angeles Times*, Maslin turned earth mother when describing Wahlberg's performance as "providing galvanizing brute force."

Bad reviews were followed by worse word of mouth when the movie opened on April 21, 1995. It landed at number 16 its opening weekend in 300 theaters, with a disappointing $714,000 three-day take and an anemic $2,380 per-screen average—the real gauge of audience enthusiasm. The distributor planned to "platform" the film, typical of art-house releases, where theaters are gradually added as positive word-of-mouth and interest grow.

Word-of-mouth, however, must have been "Stay away," because after only two months the movie fell off the charts. With a final gross of $2.1 million, the film didn't even earn back its $4 million budget, not to mention the cost of the ad campaign, which typically equals the cost of production.

As the reviews and box-office tallies came in, Wahlberg could console himself with the generous notices he received, which stood out even more amid the purplish prose used to pan the film. But even greater consolation must have been the fact that he was too busy to check out *Variety*'s weekly grosses and lethal reviews because he had already reported to the set of his next movie project. And this time he was the star!

CHAPTER 13

Matinee Idolatry

If a pheromone could talk, it would sound like Marky Mark.

—a fan too embarrassed by his enthusiasm for Mark Wahlberg to be identified by name

Fear (1996), a thriller about a psycho teen who stalks his ex-girlfriend and her family, was shot on location in Seattle, Washington, but it might as well have been heaven as far as Mark was concerned. In his first two feature films, he had been a member of ensemble casts and had proved two important things: He might be inexperienced, but he was a competent actor who could hold his own opposite major stars with much more impressive résumés than his. Even more crucial to his film career, Wahlberg's professionalism and courtly behavior on the set showed that his bad-boy act had been just that—an act. He might play a gangsta-stripper onstage, but on the soundstage he was a real trouper.

Fear represented a major career step for the twenty-five-year-old, because it was his first starring screen role. The step was also perilously slippery. There would be no ensemble to hide any acting weaknesses. *Fear* would be the Marky Mark Show, and he had to carry the movie by sheer force of talent. This time, there would be no cutting to shower scenes for comic/orgasmic relief. Wahlberg had to act, and once again, the enthusiastic reviews for his performance, if not the film, would prove that he could.

Fear showed the glimmerings of a major screen personality in the making. Robert De Niro and Dustin Hoffman are "actuhs." Brad Pitt and Denzel Washington are movie stars, a source no less authoritative than *Time* magazine once declared. With *Fear*, Wahlberg joined the Brad Pack. Before the project put him in the Pack, an open casting call took place to secure the lead player. An ad in *Drama-Logue* perfectly described the man who would eventually get the job: "Caucasian male: 18–25, must be no older than 25. Incredibly sexy, intelligent, intense. Seemingly misunderstood, poetic, lost soul whose personality transforms into an obsessive dangerous tough psychotic. Appropriate talent *only* come to an open call." A perfect description of Mark's personal and professional evolution—except in real life the transformation occurred in reverse.

The movie was produced by a major studio, Universal, with Mark's biggest movie budget to date, $14 million. It was also the first film in which he received top billing, although considering the credits of the other cast members, there wouldn't have been a creditable fight among their agents for the top spot. In this zits-and-all reinterpretation of *Fatal Attraction* (1987), Reese Witherspoon plays the sixteen-year-old "Michael Douglas" role opposite Wahlberg's "Glenn Close." Respected stage actor William Petersen plays Witherspoon's dad, a beleaguered type-A personality and architect whose obvious Oedipal attraction to his daughter is just that, and hardly fatal.

"Fatal," however, is a good way to describe Wahlberg's character's growing obsession with his girlfriend, whom he deflowers on-camera in a scene that earned the thriller an R-rating. Interestingly and by now typically, the star rips off his shirt in the sequence, and the camera wanders over the terra firma that is Mark Wahlberg like a *National Geographic* documentary. Witherspoon keeps her bra on the whole time, and the cinematographer shoots her almost absentmindedly. The casting of Witherspoon—then a neophyte with only a few feature films to her credit, *The Man in the Moon* (1991) and *S.F.W.* (1995)—was wryly questioned by one film critic. He noted that the teen was cute but not beautiful like Alicia Silverstone, who had played a similar rich-kid movie role in *Clueless* (1995).

The same critic told me but not his readers, "You get the feeling that the casting people or the studio wanted to make Marky look even hotter by pairing him with a girl who wasn't as pretty as he is!" Even the highbrow British journal *Sight and Sound* got a bit down and dirty comparing the relative allure of the two leads: "She can hardly steal scenes from boy-hunk rap artist Mark Wahlberg. All Witherspoon gets to counter Wahlberg's outrageous [body] is a couple of shower scenes." The magazine failed to mention that Witherspoon is shot from the neck up in the shower.

Much more impressive than Mark's colleagues on-screen were the people behind the camera: director James Foley, who had worked with everyone from David Mamet (*Glengarry Glen Ross,* 1992) to Madonna (*Who's That Girl?,* 1987), and super-hot producer Brian Grazer *(Apollo 13,* 1995). Foley had another credit that must have impressed and encouraged Wahlberg. He had directed Madonna's controversial video, "Papa Don't Preach," which the Christian right denounced as promoting unwed motherhood.

Wahlberg knew he would be in good hands with a director who felt equally at home in the chop-chop, quick-cut medium of music videos as well as in the slower-paced marathon of feature-filmmaking. The young actor wouldn't have to worry about condescending treatment from a director who might turn up his professional nose at MTV since he had cut his teeth in the same medium.

Despite the opportunity to star in a feature film for the first time and to work with impressive talent, Mark still feared *Fear*. He had already played a one-dimensional thug in his last effort, *The Basketball Diaries*, and now he was being asked—courted, even—to do an encore, only with more lines and even more menace onscreen. From street punk to psycho was not the career progression Wahlberg cared to make. With typical self-possession, he turned down Universal, which, typically, made the studio want him even more. To obtain his services, the filmmakers allowed the novice to change the focus of the movie from gangbangers on the loose, to a more noirish character study.

"The original idea was about a crew of guys like the Spur Posse who were doing all this messed-up shit. But I thought they were a little bit pathetic and not interesting enough. After three movies, I wasn't a master filmmaker or anything, but there were just certain things I could relate to a little bit more than Jamie [Foley] could, and obviously there were a lot of things he knew a lot more about," Wahlberg said to *Movieline* magazine in May 1997.

For a guy who professes he doesn't like to read movie scripts, Mark had done his research on director Foley. Despite misgivings about *Fear*'s crack-addled gang, who did make it into the final cut, but with fewer lines, Wahlberg wanted to work with Foley after screening his masterful direction of a Pulitzer Prize-winning play with major talents like Jack Lemmon, Al Pacino, and another stud-turned-thespian, Alec Baldwin.

"I thought Jamie Foley did an amazing job on *Glengarry Glen Ross*, and—what was the title of that other movie that was great . . . ?" (*At Close Range*, 1986, starring another bad-boy-gone-good, Sean Penn). "We were really gonna try to do it in a way it hadn't been done before. The opportunity of working with Jamie was huge at that stage of the game," Wahlberg said in his May 1997 *Movieline* interview, sounding more like an artist's manager than an artist.

Foley, an egoless filmmaker with a reputation in the business for handling hard-to-handle stars, didn't resent Wahlberg's input into the script. After the wrap, the director put the actor on his "must work with again" list. He also paid the high-school dropout the supreme compliment of comparing him to Harvard grad Jack Lemmon, considered one of the least difficult actors in Hollywood. "Every single actor is a totally different animal. *Glengarry Glen Ross* was the most illustrative of that. . . . I would have to say something to each [actor], and I would automatically change my language, because every actor has different needs. For instance, I probably talk to Mark Wahlberg very similarly to the way I would talk to Jack Lemmon, and very different than I would talk to Al Pacino," Foley told Dennis Hensley in the March 1996 issue of *Detour* magazine.

And if there were any residual fears among studio executives about Wahlberg's bad-boy rep, Foley annihilated them when he was quoted in a national magazine: "I've got to say, working with Mark really has been one of the more pleasurable experiences of my career. He's incredibly centered, has no fear, and is free of neurosis. So often there's a certain kind of power politics to the movie, and people need their importance puffed up, and Mark is absolutely free of that."

Foley sounded as though he were still recovering from the Madonna/Penn "experiences." But the director's pleasant memories of his collaboration with Mark must have put Madonna out of his mind. He told *Time*, in a major piece on the object of his praise: "[Mark] seemed to have access to a great deal of emotion with little effort. He doesn't wear his intensity on his sleeve. But he is very intense, very serious. . . . He's driven to be celebrated for the quality of his work."

It was in this atmosphere that Foley and Universal Pictures acquiesced when Mark made another demand. Adhering to writer Norman Mailer's macho rule that tough guys don't dance, Mark refused to strut his stuff, despite a pivotal scene in the script where he and Witherspoon first meet at a weird, amalgam yuppie/ biker bar.

Witherspoon described how Mark hung tough and refused to gyrate on-camera. "Originally we were supposed to do something really cheesy like 'surrender to the beat and move rhythmically,'" Witherspoon recalled, quoting the original stage directions. "But Mark refused to dance. I'm like, 'Millions have been made from your dancing,' but he didn't want to dance," she said.

And he had the clout and self-confidence to stick to his no-dance decision. "You don't know the fights I had over that shit!" he said, wisely declining to name the names of his combatants. There were other fights, and Mark won those, too. Like *Renaissance Man*, the credits reveal that Wahlberg wrote and/or performed several songs on the soundtrack. And like his movie debut, his vocal performances occur only in voice-overs and during the closing credits. He never sings on-screen.

Brian Grazer, who has produced several blockbuster pictures, didn't resent his star's refusal to trade on his rapper image, either. Grazer said, "He didn't do any of the affectations that Marky Mark had. He refused to be referred to as Marky Mark. That wasn't his identity any longer. He was inflexible about it."

Like the director and producer, Wahlberg's two leading ladies became charter members of the Marky Mark fan club. Despite allegations that they were "roughed up" by their costar, neither of the "victims" complained about the mistreatment because it was all in the service of the script. Witherspoon and costar Alyssa Milano (*Who's the Boss?*), however, may have wished their leading man had spent less time at Gold's Gym, pushing his weights around.

Witherspoon recalled, without anger, to *Detour* magazine (March 1996), "There's this scene where Mark has to grab me. He doesn't really know his own strength. I had purple-and-green bruises on my arms for two weeks. It's tough shooting this kind of movie. When you're doing a comedy, everybody comes on the set happy. This kind of movie, you wake up and you're like, 'Who's going to die today?' It's a horrible feeling."

Milano felt worse after an audition with this fledgling actor whose method seemed like madness. For the March 1996 issue of *Detour,* Milano described her close encounter of the turgid kind with Mark, after being fortified with booze supplied by the studio: "At this point, I've had three beers—I'm 97 pounds, so I'm a nervous wreck. So I go in. Jamie [Foley] says, 'Roll the camera as soon as Mark comes in.' So Mark comes barreling through the door, shoves me against the wall, is screaming at me. All of a sudden I start crying, which I've never done at an audition in my life. I always fake it. I'm wearing a tight little sweater, and Mark goes to grab my face and pulls my sweater up by accident, and I'm wearing no bra, the camera's going, and I'm freaking out. I was really glad I'd had those beers. Do I go on?"

A trouper, Milano pushed Wahlberg away, something the script did *not* call for, and went on with the screen test. In his defense, it should be noted that Wahlberg wasn't overacting. The same scene, only much more violent and sexually explicit, occurs in the final cut of *Fear*. Mark wasn't following a natural inclination; he was following the script. Even so, Wahlberg showed his true feelings—big-time guilt—as soon as the audition ended. Milano said, "When it was over, Mark fell to the floor and said, 'I'm *sooooo* sorry.'"

Like Witherspoon and Foley, Milano found that she, too, enjoyed the collaboration, despite the hazardous interaction. The audition "was so traumatic, but I'm glad I went through it, because it's definitely worth it!" the former sitcom star said of her first major feature film.

Later Milano would reveal that their screen test wasn't the only time Mark got carried away, but again she attributed it to inexperience and enthusiasm, not attitude. "Because he hasn't been acting very long," said Milano— a veteran of eight seasons on TV's *Who's the Boss?*—"he doesn't understand yet how to pull hair for a scene without it hurting. I had these welts on the back of my head, and no matter how many times you'd tell him, he'd just get so caught up in the take that he couldn't help it."

Just like the audition, as soon as the director yelled cut, Wahlberg screamed, "I'm sorry!" "He felt so bad about it," Milano told *Detour* magazine. "He felt terrible. He'd come over and go, 'I'm so sorry, baby.' He'd bring me a soda and be like, 'You okay?' In the midst of a very inhuman business, to have someone care about you like that was very human."

Despite a grueling shoot and stunts that left him bruised, Wahlberg would have agreed with Milano that *Fear* was "definitely worth it," too. The film not only revealed a newly minted matinee idol, but a serious actor with a knack for accents. In real life, if such a thing exists in Hollywood, Mark still speaks with a pronounced Boston accent, swallowing his *r*'s with big gulps. A film critic for the *L.A. Weekly* carped that, despite *Fear*'s Seattle setting, Wahlberg sounded as though he were still "pahking his car in the Hahvuhd yahd." The reviewer must have been watching another film when he noted, "Wahlberg's thick vowels clinch [the character's] lumpen pedigree."

Actually, Mark's speaking voice in *Fear* is magnificent—and his Boston accent is undetectable! By now the rapper spoke on-camera with a whiskey-soaked whisper deepened by a three-pack-a-day cigarette habit. His blue-collar accent had vanished. Physically, there was a new Mark on-screen, too. His torso shows that you can indeed improve on perfection, since he's even hunkier here than in his musical heyday. The baby fat (face only) has also gone, and the phrase "chiseled good looks" doesn't even begin to describe his transformation into a WASP Valentino.

While the director of *Fear* couldn't resist flashing some Wahlberg flesh on-screen, he satirizes Mark's bimbo past by "vandalizing" the living billboard even more grotesquely than the Sunset Strip taggers had when they threw garbage at the huge display. In one of many on-screen scenes that are painful to watch, Mark carves the inscription "Nicole 4 Evuh" into those perfect pecs and abs, then smears ink from a ballpoint pen into the wound to create a permanent tattoo. *Sight and Sound* wryly noted that Mark's inscription might have been a sly reference to a real-life tattoo—"Winona Forever!"—that Johnny Depp inflicted on his deltoid while dating the star of *The Age of Innocence* (1991).

Universal put its formidable publicity machine and distribution system behind *Fear*. Perhaps too much publicity. The movie had originally been titled *No Fear*, which also happens to be the name of a major apparel manufacturer. Universal did such a good job creating pre-release publicity for the picture, that No Fear's brass got wind of the usage and didn't like the smell. During the first week of shooting in Vancouver, Universal received a cease-and-desist order from the clothier's attorneys. The designer label didn't want to be associated with a movie about crack addicts who behead the family dog, then shove Fido's face through the doggie door.

Bryan Friedman, No Fear's attorney, said, "This isn't a *Side Out*"—a film about a volleyball team and a manufacturer of the same name. "*No Fear* isn't about anything we'd like to be associated with. My guys don't want money. They just want the title changed or the film stopped."

Universal wasn't about to halt a multimillion production over something as simple as a two-letter word. The title was quietly changed to *Fear*, which in retrospect was a much better description of the emotion Wahlberg's gentleman brawler inspires on the big screen.

The studio had high hopes for the production and opened it "wide" on April 22, 1996, in 1,584 theaters, a relatively blockbuster-size number of screens. The film debuted in fourth place, a respectable showing for a release without a big-name star to "open" it.

According to CinemaScore, the box-office survey service, the theaters were largely filled with females: sixty-three percent, to be exact. Sixty percent of them were under twenty-five and probably carrying a copy of *Tiger Beat* or *Sassy* under their arm. Moviegoers who described themselves as "couldn't wait to see the movie" by CinemaScore, gave *Fear* an A-minus. Surprisingly, those who said they "were drawn by Mark Wahlberg" to turn up opening weekend, only gave the film a B-plus! Maybe they didn't like their idol defacing himself in the do-it-yourself tattoo scene.

The critics gave *Fear*, the movie, an F. However, the same reviewers awarded Mark, the actor, an A! *Entertainment Today* said, "Wahlberg takes a good stab at the impossible role he's been given to play, seeming convincingly amorous and menacing." *Movieline* wrote that *Fear* was better than *Cape Fear,* and suggested a remake with Wahlberg in the De Niro role even though *Cape* had been released only five years earlier. "*Fear* is more satisfying than *Cape Fear* because Wahlberg is a more cuddly villain than De Niro."

The *New York Times'* Stephen Holden enthused, "Surprise, surprise. Mark Wahlberg, the pug-faced actor formerly known as Marky Mark, could be on the verge of full-fledged movie stardom . . . oozing a seductive sexual menace. . . . With his slit eyes, working-class accent and feline stealth, Mr. Wahlberg conjures up images of the young John Garfield and Robert Ryan in their more unsavory roles, although he is much more boyish than either." Holden's colleague at the *Times'* Sunday *Magazine*, Frank Bruni, reported, "Wahlberg got to play florid evil and delivered a seductive, scene-stealing performance."

Entertainment Weekly, like most of the CinemaScorers, gave *Fear* a B, but upgraded its opinion of the star, whom it called a "danger-zone stud," adding, "Wahlberg gives a genuine performance." The *Los Angeles Daily News* and the *Hollywood Reporter* judged Mark a "convincing monster," and meant it as a compliment. *Variety* paid him the same compliment, even using the same term: Witherspoon is "strongly supported by Wahlberg, who's quite convincing as the gentleman caller from hell."

The only negative voice in the chorus of hallelujahs came from Jack Matthews, the critic for New York's *Newsday*. After seeing *Fear*, Matthews wasn't feeling very generous: "The film's problems revolve around Wahlberg. The model and former hip-hop artist is good at miming psychopathic evil. He has a stare that will melt steel. But it's like a big joke on the audience that Nicole (Witherspoon) looks at him from across the room and sees a dreamboat."

Instead of this "dreamboat," Matthews saw the human equivalent of the *Titanic*, a disaster waiting to happen. "What we see looks like a paroled sex offender, one who did not ask to be castrated before his release. [Wahlberg's] voice, a sort of whispered sleaziness . . . makes him more comical than menacing."

The *Hollywood Reporter* predicted *Fear* would be a sleeper hit, but in fact it ended up as a relative disappointment, grossing only $20 million in the U.S. and Canada. However, since its budget was reportedly a mere $14 million, Universal must have been happy and not averse to working with Wahlberg again.

Except that the adventurous actor had other acting plans, and they didn't include cloning himself in another big-studio, demographics-driven teen pic. Next up for Wahlberg would be a project both low-budget and *very* independent.

CHAPTER 14

Grifting, Not Drifting

Between acting in *Twister* (1996), which grossed $246 million in the U.S. and Canada alone, and *Titanic* (1997), at nearly a billion dollars and still floating, actor Bill Paxton required a little soul food for a spirit malnourished on junk-food movies. These popcorn epics made more than enough money to provide him with the industry clout to produce a small, character-driven movie to showcase talent capable of playing opposite something more challenging than a mile-high funnel or sinking ocean liner. In *Traveller* (1997), he found the perfect script for his needs. It dealt with a clan of real-life Scots-Irish con men who roam the South. After *Twister* blew people out of the theaters, Paxton easily found the $4 million to finance his project. His "angel" was the tiny independent production company, October Films.

The star/auteur described his newfound clout perfectly: "I've always wanted to produce but have never been in a position politically to do it before. Because of the recent films I've been in, I can now set up an independent film," he said a month before the project began principal photography in Wilmington, North Carolina, on November 29, 1995. Shot on the run and on the cheap, production wrapped in TV-movie speed of only thirty-five days.

Paxton loved the script by Nichols Award-winner Jim McGlynn so much, he turned down director James Brooks (*As Good As It Gets*) when Brooks offered him a role in *The Evening Star* (1996), a sequel to the Oscar-winning *Terms of Endearment* (1983). (Paxton was so hot, however, Brooks postponed *The Evening Star* until the actor finished *Traveller*.)

In *Traveller*, Paxton plays Bokky, a scummy grifter whose specialty is impersonating an asphalt resurfacer. In an early scene, he shows up at the home of a target with the riff that he's just sealed someone else's driveway, has sealant left over, and it's about to go to waste. For a rock-bottom price, he will spray tar over the cracks in the homeowner's driveway. The price and the deal sound too good to be true. The luckless victims fork over $300, then rave about what a marvelous job has been done protecting the asphalt against rain damage. As Paxton's Bokky pulls away in his truck, it begins to rain, and the "sealant" dissolves instantly, as indelible as pastel watercolor!

With a muscular résumé pumped up by such action films as *Aliens* (1986), *True Lies* (1994), and *Apollo 13* (1995), Paxton now sought professional respect and spiritual nourishment. In contrast, it's hard to figure out, at first blush, what Mark Wahlberg was after when he signed on to play a screen role which received second billing in the credits and was a distant second in importance to Paxton's screen lead. The *New York Times Magazine* called *Traveller* an art-house movie, a weird term for a film with lots of action and ultraviolence. Maybe it was the tiny budget that misled the magazine, which described *Traveller* as an "arty character-study about Southern con men that accentuated [Wahlberg's] aura as an actor more concerned with his work than his wallet."

Sometimes it seemed Wahlberg didn't even carry a wallet, figuratively speaking. The same year he said yes to a supporting role in a low-budget film, he said no to Paul Verhoeven, the director who had made Sharon Stone a star in *Basic Instinct* (1992). Verhoeven offered him the lead in *Starship Troopers* (1997) at a time when everyone in the movie industry was obsessed with extraterrestrials and the box office they generated. *Independence Day* had been the number one hit of 1996. Perhaps Wahlberg didn't read *Daily Variety* before he met with the Dutch-born director. "I went in on a meeting and then got the hell out of there. I just don't know if I could say, 'Let's stomp those conqueror-roaches!' I *coulda* done it. But would I be able to look myself in the mirror afterward?" Mark said in the June 1997 issue of *Movieline* magazine.

Not fearing whose toes he stepped on, even a powerful director like Verhoeven's, Wahlberg profanely dissed the project at length in the same *Movieline* piece. "I don't go to fuckin' space running around with Martians and shit. I can't look at a blue screen and say, you know, 'These bugs are gonna fuckin' kill us, man!' Maybe down the line when I start getting a little bit more mechanical, it probably wouldn't be as hard because by then I probably wouldn't give a shit. But I don't want to get to that point."

To date and to his credit, Wahlberg's choice of projects shows he's nowhere near a point of sale. "I just have to be patient, go up for a thing I'm right for and hope for the opportunity to be in a good movie." (Casper Van Dien, a relative unknown, starred in *Starship Troopers*, which only did modest business at the box office despite expectations for such a high-concept movie. Once again, Mark showed he could sniff out a stinker.)

Not that he turned his nose up at *good* popcorn movies. Mark really wanted to play Robin in *Batman Forever* (1995). But the role of Robin went to Chris O'Donnell, an actor with a slightly better résumé but a much lower stud-quotient for the all-important female teen audience.

In *Traveller*, Mark plays Pat, an unemployed youth who brings his father's body home to the South for burial. With coffin in tow, he's driven to the encampment of his dad's relatives, called "Travellers" (a secret society/religious sect that breeds and raises con people). His father had been kicked out of the family before Pat was born for marrying outside the clan. His white-trash relatives consider Mark an untouchable, and after the cemetery service, the head of the clan tells him to get lost. (In these early scenes, Wahlberg once again shows what a terrific actor he is. Those who would later consider his acting skills in *Boogie Nights* such a revelation apparently never saw his previous movies.)

The look of utter desolation mixed with financial panic on Mark's face when Boss Jack, the Travellers' leader, tells him to beat it, explains why within a year critics would be falling all over themselves for adjectives to praise his performance in the more widely seen *Boogie Nights*.

Early on in the film, it becomes clear why Wahlberg accepted second billing in *Traveller* and agreed to work below scale (the film was non-union). *Traveller* is as much a character study of Pat (Wahlberg) as it is of Bokky (Paxton). This film also allowed Wahlberg to escape on-camera typecasting as a thug. Here, he's a naïf who falls into the company of human wolves, who not only eat Grandma but Little Red Riding Hood, too. His G-rated romance with a pretty cousin—played by Nikki DeLoach—that never gets beyond a few kisses, also may have attracted him after *Fear*'s R-rated "romance" scenes.

Then, partway through the film a funny thing happens in the story line of *Traveller*. Wahlberg inexplicably becomes as corrupt and callous as his "cousins." A running scam in the movie has Paxton and Wahlberg reselling a Winnebago they don't own. In one horrific scene, a woman who looks ten months' pregnant begs to buy the trailer because she has no place to live. She only has nine thousand dollars, and the asking price is ten. By now, Paxton's multidimensional character is developing a conscience and offers to let the woman have the van for seven thousand! Mark interrupts and demands full price. If Wahlberg took a pay cut to escape his thuggish screen past,

Traveller was not the project with which to make the great escape. And as for character evolution, there is little solid motivation for his drift into grift since he was not even brought up in the subculture.

At least this time around, there were no fights over Wahlberg's participation as a rap artist. The film's soundtrack is pure country music, and Wahlberg didn't feel the need to stretch musically. As producer, Paxton ordered up a catalog of tunes by his favorite country artists. The bill for song clearances came to $400,000, and the distributor, October Films, would not approve such costs. As a result, Paxton ended up using only Al Green's "Love and Happiness" and over the opening credits a very expensive cover by country superstar Randy Travis, doing the Roger Miller chestnut, "King of the Road."

If Wahlberg took a pay cut in *Traveller* hoping for good reviews, he got a bargain. Once again, the critics loved Mark, hated the picture. Paxton also earned rave notices as an actor, but as a producer he must have cringed when he read the critics' reviews.

Peter Rainer, *New Times'* urban-guerrilla film critic, said that a ten-minute segment on TV's *Dateline* provided more information than all of *Traveller*'s one hundred minutes. But like his colleagues, Rainer praised Paxton's generosity toward the rest of the cast: Paxton "[is] such a generous performer that he shines a light on his costars."

Other reviewers enthused over Wahlberg's performance; some drooled over him as well. Amy Taubin sounded like a *Tiger Beat* subscriber, not the hip critic for the *Village Voice*, when she wrote, "Tough, sexy, and looking more than ever like a fireplug, Mark Wahlberg has the thankless job of playing sidekick to a star whose attention is inexplicably elsewhere. . . . Wahlberg rises to the non-occasion. He's the best thing in the movie." *L.A. Weekly* said, "Wahlberg is developing into something of an actor." The *New York Times'* Janet Maslin felt Mark was working too hard at being a serious actor in *Traveller*. But at least he didn't "mumble his way through the film the way so many of his peers like Keanu Reeves and Brad Pitt do like young incarnations of Warren Beatty," Maslin said.

The only negative vote against Mark wasn't even cast in a review. A year and a half after its release, Peter Travers wrote in a "think piece" for *US* magazine, "*Traveller* was a good movie. Oddly enough, Wahlberg's timing was off in the role of a gypsy con man in training. It's as if the actor hadn't yet come to terms with his character."

Favorable reviews couldn't compensate, however, for the film's box-office performance. *Traveller* was clearly one for the actor's résumé, not the record books. It opened on April 18, 1997, in only six theaters. October Films may have planned to platform *Traveller*, letting word of mouth grow and then adding new theaters accordingly. More likely, made on a shoestring and released with a microscopic advertising budget, *Traveller* ended up in only half a dozen movie houses because October Films couldn't afford a wider distribution and the cost of thousands of prints.

Although it received mixed reviews, *Traveller* grossed $30,805 in its opening weekend for an impressive $5,134 per-screen average. Unfortunately, after a full week in release, the total had reached only an anemic $43,857. A month and a half later, *Traveller* fell off the box-office charts faster than Wahlberg's second album had. The cumulative gross was a meager $511,633. (It didn't help that October Films never showed the movie in more than sixty-three theaters throughout the United States!)

However, like the fallout from *Fear*, by the time the bad box-office news about *Traveller* reached Wahlberg, he was already immersed in a new project which would make him an A-list actor and wrest the title "De Niro of his generation" away from buddy/rival Leonardo DiCaprio. Unfortunately, Wahlberg wasn't out of town and far away from industry snickers when *Traveller*'s paltry grosses were published in the Hollywood trade papers. He was right over the hill in another kind of hell, the San Fernando Valley, in the middle of a subtropical heat wave.

Despite the humidity and location, beautiful downtown Reseda, Wahlberg knew for certain "everything would be cool, man." Except for his career, which was about to get *very* hot!

CHAPTER 15

The Heartbreak of Satyriasis

Mark Wahlberg came to me and said,"I've got an inch on Leo," and he showed it to me, so I hired him instead.

—*Boogie Nights* (1997) director Paul Thomas Anderson, on why he changed his mind about casting Leonardo DiCaprio as porn star Dirk Diggler

Boogie Nights takes an anthropological look at the porn industry during the late 1970s and early 1980s. The ensemble cast, which includes Burt Reynolds, Julianne Moore, and Wahlberg, toils in the flesh factory of the triple-X film-within-a-film format of *Boogie Nights*. The *New York Times* perhaps summarized the plot best: "In the course of the two-and-a-half-hour epic, Wahlberg's porn star, Dirk Diggler, masturbates for money, has on-camera sex, snorts coke, robs houses and delivers a monologue with a thirteen-inch fake penis hanging between his legs."

When Wahlberg heard what went on in the pages of *Boogie Nights*, he almost passed on the project without bothering to read the script. Nudity, thuggery, drug use—they were exactly the things he wanted to distance himself from in his screen career and personal history. As a concept, *Boogie Nights* reminded him of "all the stuff I wanted to get away from. My past, making a fool of myself. . . . The whole subject matter kind of turned me off in the initial stages," he told David Ansen in the October 6, 1997, issue of *Newsweek* magazine.

The climactic scene, in which the "hero" does a monologue with full frontal nudity, unheard-of for a male star in a mainstream movie, particularly disturbed him.

In the original script, there were actually several scenes that called for the porn star to drop his drawers, and this time Wahlberg wouldn't be wearing Calvins or anything else underneath. Besides the obvious objection to acting in the nude, the scenes raised the problem of credibility. Everyone had seen Wahlberg in the Klein ads and could tell he didn't have Dirk's sole "talent."

"There were at least three big scenes in the film that required the character to strip down and reveal his impressive endowment," Mark said. He called the director, Paul Thomas Anderson, and summarily rejected the role. "I'm definitely not your man. I asked him if he'd seen my underwear ads. If so, he'd have realized I'd never have been able to hide something like that in a pair of Calvin Kleins," he told Ivor Davis of the *New York Times* Syndicate (November 1997).

The actor also worried about being identified too closely with the role and the character's biggest claim to fame. Those who hadn't seen his underwear ads might think "it" was the real thing. "If I did the movie with the prosthetic penis, there were obviously going to be people who believed it was all me. That meant two things. I'd probably get followed into a lot of washrooms, and girls I'd date in the future would have enormous expectations," he said in the *New York Times* Syndicate interview.

The project possibly scared him, too. A cheeky lunch date asked Mark if the script didn't make him fear the fate of Elizabeth Berkley, another novice who destroyed her career in the horrifically risible *Showgirls* (1995), a film whose subculture of Las Vegas strippers was actually classier than *Boogie Nights*' sex workers. *Movieline* magazine's Stephen Rebello asked Wahlberg during lunch at the Four Seasons in Los Angeles "why he chose to do a movie from which it must have seemed he could easily emerge as the male Elizabeth Berkley, instead of the daring, serious actor he wants to prove himself to be."

Instead of punching out his interrogator, Wahlberg whispered this answer: "When I read this script, I was like, 'Either they're going to make me the underwear-boy-embarrassment-most-pathetic-piece-of-shit-in-the-world, or this movie is going to be brilliant.' I wanted to be good in a good movie. I wanted to do something totally different, to prove to people that, in the right situation, I *can* act. I've gotta play different parts or I might as well just get on a TV show. This felt like a movie that the filmmakers were going to make because they felt it *should* be made. And why I loved it so much is that I believe in it too. Somebody could tell me it's the worst thing in the world and I'd be like, 'What are you talking about?' I don't really care what anybody else thinks."

As usual, Wahlberg hadn't read the script when he'd turned up his nose at the idea of playing a porn star. Reading the screenplay helped change his mind; but just like his meeting with Penny Marshall for *Renaissance Man*, a chat with the director, twenty-six-year-old Paul Thomas Anderson, made him a believer, even a cheerleader for the project. (Actually, there were two crucial chats. The first one, on the phone, turned off the director. The second, in person, marked the beginning of a friendship that continues to this day.)

Anderson admits that Wahlberg was not his first choice for the lead. Leonardo DiCaprio had turned him down, but not because of the controversial subject. Leo, as his buds call him, was busy making a movie about some ship sinking in the North Atlantic. (Wahlberg joked that the only reason he got the job was that his endowment was more impressive than DiCaprio's. The director later changed his story about his casting decision and claimed, "Mark . . . came to me and said, 'I've got an inch on Leo.' And he showed it to me, so I hired him instead,'" as reported by Matt Hendrickson in the April 2, 1998, issue of *Rolling Stone*.)

Anderson recalled his first impression of Wahlberg after meeting on the phone. "I said, 'All right, what do you think of the script?' And he said, 'Well, to tell the truth, I've only read thirty pages.' I was like, Who the hell does this guy think he is? He said, 'I've got a problem. I like it so much, but I need to know before I keep reading: Do you want me because I'm the guy who'll get down to his underwear?' I said, 'No, I don't know anything about that. I'm meeting you because you're an actor, and I loved you in *Basketball Diaries*!'"

Despite the compliment, which was based on his screenwork rather than on his workouts, Wahlberg didn't exactly rush to take a meeting with Anderson. Instead, he said, "Great! Can I call you back after I finish reading it?"

According to Jan Stuart (*Los Angeles Times*, November 1, 1997), Anderson remembered thinking, but not saying, What a jerk! Fortunately, while first impressions can be the strongest, they aren't always the most lasting. Post-production, the director (in *Rolling Stone*, October 30, 1997) sounded more like someone accessing the Marky Mark fan club Web site: "Mark is a great actor. He's just great, fucking great. That's kinda how I feel about Mark. I love him."

In reality, the actor's hesitancy about reading the screenplay didn't reflect disrespect or laziness. The subject matter scared him—and that was after only thirty pages! "In the first thirty pages, there were two things I never wanted to do on-screen. One was dance. The other was take my clothes off," Mark said. Despite the blandishments of powerful studio execs and directors he adored, Wahlberg had done neither in his previous movies. "I felt that if it went wrong, all the Marky Mark shit would come back and haunt me," he told Garth Pearce in the London *Sunday Times* (January 11, 1998).

Wahlberg also feared that a well-written script might seduce him into signing on to a project that would reinforce his beefcake image and remind the public of his personal problems in the past. "If it's not something I'm interested in, then I don't even really want to get into the material, because the material could change my opinion and make me overlook what's most important to me at the end of the day—which is doing something great and different as an actor," he explained.

Despite his misgivings, Mark found he couldn't put the script down. And yet he still hadn't finished it before meeting the director. Wahlberg is a very slow reader. As he crawled through the 260-page script, he thought, "God, I've got to meet the guy who wrote the film and is going to direct it. I thought, for better or for worse, I have to meet him; then I'll know what he's going after."

Another reason he didn't finish the script was that the first part was so well conceived he feared the remainder would "turn to shit," he recalled post-production.

With some impressive filmwork under his belt, Wahlberg went to the meeting with an attitude. He loved the script, but his attitude seemed to be to "wait and see" what the director was really like. Maybe it was the sight of a kid a year *younger* than himself that made him drop the deference he usually showed more experienced pros. Seventies sitcom stars and role models like Penny Marshall and Danny DeVito commanded respect bordering on idolization. The twenty-something director sitting across from him didn't have the cultural resonance for Mark that someone like Laverne DeFazio or Louie Di Palma did.

Instead of breaking the ice with something like, "Hello, whassup?" Wahlberg began the conversation with a blunt question: "Is it about the Marky Mark thing?"

Anderson was a good salesman. After making only one film, the barely distributed *Hard Eight* (1997), the director convinced New Line Cinema to bankroll his new script about such an untouchable subject as people who engage in public sex for money. With the same skills he used to convince New Line, Anderson sold his reluctant star on the project. "It took five minutes of talking," Wahlberg said. "There were so many positives. The screenplay was phenomenal," he said in *Newsweek* (October 6, 1997).

Although it took the director a bit longer to warm up, for Mark it was admiration at first chat. "I met him, and I just fell in love with him. I thought he was genuinely interested in me as an actor." One industry source suggested the director became a "surrogate younger brother to Wahlberg," an analogy based more on chronological age than on the more usual relationship of father-son bonding between director and actor. Whatever the familial connection, during a joint interview to promote the movie, they did indeed act like siblings, although Anderson came from an affluent family. Unlike the absent Wahlberg Senior, Paul's father, Ernie Anderson, was a well-paid voice-over announcer and TV horror-show host. Despite the differences in their socioeconomic backgrounds, the artistic collaboration turned into a genuine off-soundstage friendship. By way of a greeting during an interview in a tacky Hollywood bar, Anderson punched his star's bicep and chanted, "Marky! Marky!" Wahlberg hated the reference to his rap past more than the punch, but didn't object to either. You have to be a *very* good friend to get away with punching Wahlberg. As for their relationship on the soundstage, Wahlberg said, "I just put myself in the hands of the PTA."

Director Anderson said appreciatively of his star: "Forget the Marky Mark shit, forget the underwear shit, that's boring and old. This is a fucking great, Sean Penn-type performance [in *Boogie Nights*]. Nothing against Leonardo DiCaprio, who was *almost* in this movie, but Mark is better than Leonardo would have been. It's clear Mark will do anything in a movie. He's not a movie star, because movie stars are usually embarrassed. He's an actor. He's going to get great scripts now. Great directors are going to want to work with him."

The working relationship between Wahlberg and Anderson also prospered because both men shared the screenwriter's anthropological take on a "culture" that could have been given the Paul Schrader-*Hardcore* (1979) treatment of repulsion/attraction, guilt and lust: Isn't this terrible? Now let's watch two and a half more hours of it!

Instead, Wahlberg identified the porno collective as a "tribe" that fulfilled one another's needs and dreams. "I think America *needs Boogie Nights.* It's about very human people trying to build a sense of family, to repair their mistakes, to fulfill their dreams—just like everybody else. What somebody does for a living doesn't set their human worth," he told Ric Leyva of the Associated Press on November 5, 1997.

There's a slight defensiveness in his take on *Boogie Nights*' collection of softhearted hard-core sad sacks. What he really seemed to be saying is, Whether "somebody" is having intercourse in front of a movie crew or merely dropping his jeans in concert "for a living," don't judge me or Dirk.

The script was indeed a phenomenon that managed to treat a sensationalistic subject with sensitivity and affection instead of condescension and heavy breathing. *Boogie Nights* might be about visual panderers, but it never panders to its audience. More important for Wahlberg, it didn't try to continue the fleshploitation he still found himself fighting in the industry and in media interviews with reporters whose questions he felt amounted to sexual harassment, celebrity style.

Reading the script, when he finally got around to it, must have aroused contradictory feelings in the young man. The film contained many elements that seemed autobiographical. And the hero's fate could easily have been Mark's with a few career missteps and without a redemptive angel like Emily.

In *Boogie Nights*, Wahlberg is Eddie Adams (before he takes the *nom de porn* Dirk Diggler), seventeen, a high-school dropout, with no career prospects or future. He's in a dead-end job, a dishwasher in a Reseda, California, restaurant. (Mark, of course, is also diploma-less, and his last job before rap stardom was driving a tow truck.) Eddie is still living at home with mom (Joanna Gleason), a hellacious alcoholic who objects to every aspect of her son's life, from his low-status job to his "slut of a girlfriend."

One night, as he fills a steaming dishwasher in the restaurant kitchen, a chance meeting changes Eddie Adams' life. It's *A Star Is*

Born moment shot through a funhouse mirror, except no one is laughing. Adult-film auteur Jack Horner, Burt Reynolds in an Oscar-nominated performance, "discovers" Eddie bussing tables and follows him into the kitchen. Horner knows real "talent" when he sees it, and he's just had an eyeful of the view south of Eddie's belt. Horner praises Eddie, who instantly mistakes him for a john. He offers Horner a price list: "Five bucks to look, ten to touch" the object of Reynolds' praise, Eddie says, all business and commendably entrepreneurial.

Horner is not a john. He's not even gay. Horner feels comfortable enough with his own heterosexual identity to offer another man a compliment, especially when the other guy has all it takes to be a really *big* star in Horner's branch of the movie business; or, as Reynolds bullishly puts it, "There's something wonderful waiting to get out of those jeans!"

The first ninety minutes of *Boogie Nights* is a fun look at a subculture most people never get a peak at except for the finished product on video. Eddie's dizzying rise from minimum-wage slave to porn superstar has the flavor of backstage classics like *42nd Street* and *A Star Is Born*, plus the added treat of lots of flesh and explicit sex that stops just short of penetration.

The term "anthropological" was applied to the movie by so many admiring critics because the writer-director takes a dispassionate, almost scientific look at a world that may seem as alien to middle-class folks as a tribe in Equatorial Africa with a similar lack of modesty about exposing various body parts.

Dedicated armchair anthropologists, the cast felt obliged to do "field research." They made a trip to the set of an adult film, which, typically, was being shot in a private home. Because the home is often the producer's or director's, it's cheaper than a soundstage rental. This "soundstage" was in residential Hollywood Hills.

Mark recalled this particular bit of research with amusement. "The guy in the porn film was so excited to meet Burt Reynolds and Julianne Moore that he could not, uh, perform. Everyone on his film crew was giving him a tough time, and the girl involved was trying to help him, while being offended at his apparent lack of interest. In the end, we were asked to leave. It was for the best. The guy had been a fan of Marky Mark, too." The porn star's affection for Klein's poster boy may have explained the real reason for his failure to get it up on cue.

Actor Wahlberg tried hard to reserve judgment so he could interpret his character with affection, but moralist Mark was grossed out by the experience in the Hollywood Hills. "It was pretty weird, to tell the truth," he said in the London *Sunday Times* (January 11, 1998). "There were two married couples and the men were talking about sports. One says, 'Oh, I have to go and do a sex scene with your wife now.' The other guy says, 'Great. We'll talk some more when you get back.'

"It is such an unreal atmosphere, and it's something I know I could never do. I still think sex is something to be shared between two people, in private," he said.

Nevertheless, Mark found himself simulating sex in front of a gaping camera crew. Fortunately, Julianne Moore, his leading lady in the film and the video-within-the-film, was as nurturing as her screen character, who plays den mother to this substitute porn family.

"Despite my image, sex has always been a very private thing for me. Here I was having to bump and grind with Julianne. We were completely naked with all these crew people standing around watching. Julianne is one of the sweetest, nicest people on earth and what happened for me on that first day is essentially what happens in the actual scenes. She talked to me as if I were her little brother and assured me that this was the most natural thing on earth for actors. She could tell I was nervous and embarrassed," he told Ivor Davis of the *New York Times* Syndicate.

Moore was just as charmed by her costar's up-front affection. After the first script reading by the cast, Moore admitted she felt a bit uncomfortable making chitchat with a man she knew she would soon be simulating hard-core sex with. Mark, the novice, immediately put the veteran actress at ease with a blunt expression of his feelings about her.

"We were introducing ourselves to each other, and Mark and I were standing in a kitchen getting coffee, and we didn't know what to say. It was kind of awkward. And then he just looked at me and said, 'You're really nice.' I melted. I can't explain it. It was a lovely moment," Moore explained in *Premiere* magazine (May 1998).

You wonder how Moore decided simulating sex was so "natural," since her last role had been playing a middle-class pregnant wife in *Nine Months* (1995). *Boogie Nights* was also her first foray into the subject of triple-X filmmaking.

Wahlberg didn't let his own reservations about real-life porn actors affect his own performance. He plays his character wide-eyed and innocent rather than narrow-minded and jaded as he enters the murky world of porn. Burt Reynolds' character, Horner, introduces his protégé to this new world at a lavish party studded with gorgeous female porn stars willing to exchange favors for a bit of cocaine. Eddie becomes a willing participant in Horner's seduction. There he meets his future colleagues, a dreary assortment of drugs addicts, cuckolds, closeted gays, and high-school dropouts who can't get it together to pass the GED, either.

Real-life porn starlet Nina Hartley plays an actress who likes to have public sex with other men in front of her husband. (She's doing it doggie-style in the living room at the party where Eddie first meets the gang.) Like the overall progression of the story, these scenes of flagrant infidelity and exhibitionism start out funny and end in a bloodbath.

Julianne Moore, also an Oscar nominee for her work in *Boogie Nights,* plays the den mother-seductress of the group with a maternal sexiness that is painful to watch. As she has sex with Eddie and just about everybody else in the film, Moore's Amber Waves says things like, "I'm your mother . . . I love you, sonny!"

Amber "adopts" both Eddie, who desperately needs a mother figure after his own mom drives him from the house in an alcoholic rage, and Rollergirl (Heather Graham), a high-school flunkout who will do anything on-camera except remove her skates. The august London *Sunday Times* deliciously labeled her "the fetishistic Rollergirl." The almost unwatchable scene in which she stomps on the face of a "difficult" costar with her skate wheels still spinning is one of the most brutal in recent film history.

In a more tender moment, Rollergirl asks Amber if she can call her "Mom." Amber says yes immediately, even though the two will eventually participate in that staple of hetero skinflicks, lesbian sex.

Eddie takes the screen name Dirk Diggler and becomes a major figure in the turn of the 1970s-1980s era when AIDS was merely an alternate spelling for a non-prescription diet pill. Eddie also becomes rich, and his climb up the socioeconomic ladder is shot in a montage of increasing material wealth that seems as seductive to the viewer as it must be to real-life lowlifes who achieve similar success in the porn industry.

As they did in a less pathological way in Wahlberg's own rise as a rapper, fame and fortune go to Eddie's head. And a lot of coke goes up his nose. As the porn-film industry, with its arty pretensions, descends into the cheaper medium of videotape at the dawn of the Decade of Greed, Eddie's life begins a similar descent. Cocaine not only takes away his money, it robs him of his sexual "motivation." In a genuine case of worker disability, Eddie becomes impotent. And if that's not enough of a career-killer, his substance abuse makes him such a cranky diva, even Reynolds' paternalistic Jack Horner banishes him from the set and the industry—not to mention Reynolds' tacky San Fernando Valley home, which looks as though it was furnished by the Partridge Family's decorator tweaking on coke.

At this point, *Boogie Nights* shifts gears from a rollicking *A Star Is Porn* to something the early Gus Van Sant might have adapted and updated from a classic Russian novel. Eddie hits the lower depths. Broke and desperate for drugs, the raging heterosexual turns to street prostitution, but again, worker's disability thwarts this career retooling. Plus, one of his johns turns out to be a fag-basher, not a paying customer. After impotent Eddie fails to satisfy the bogus client, a pickup truck bristling with bat-wielding accomplices pulls up. They stomp on Eddie in a scene that must have revived buried memories of Mark's own teenage past in Boston.

Since prostitution obviously isn't an option, Eddie tries to reinvent himself as a pop singer. In his previous films, Wahlberg adamantly refused to rap or dance on-screen and cash in on his music stardom. In *Boogie Nights*, there were no arguments with the writer-director because Wahlberg is trashing his image, not trading on it, when he gives an excruciating performance as a singer who, like the former rap star playing him, can't sing.

For the *New York Times* Syndicate reporter, Anderson wryly responded to the question, "How did you get Mark Wahlberg to sing so badly with 'Feel the Heat' and 'You Got the Touch'?" by saying, "I asked him to sing the *best* he could, and he delivered."

For the first time in his film career, Wahlberg did a trio of things he had refused to do previously: sing, strip, and dance. As he explained to the *New York Times* Syndicate, "In almost every other movie I've done to date, or the ones I said no to, they wanted me to do these three things. Poor Dirk can't really sing. He tries it when he's trying to break away from the porn business. When he's dancing in the disco he thinks he's John Travolta. I thought that was really cool. I wasn't dancing. It was Dirk."

Even more profoundly, *Boogie Nights* allowed the emerging star to trash his other image, the pumped-up poster boy. In the 1970s, men in adult films, as adult film star Veronica Hart told me in 1983, were typically "nothing more than props. Nobody goes to erotic films to see the guys." Since the target audience for hetero porn is obviously hetero men, it didn't really matter what the guys on-screen looked like. So major "stars" like John Holmes ranged from pasty to pudgy. In keeping with its historical accuracy, *Boogie*

Nights presents Dirk as a skinny cokehead too tweaked to pump iron. To that end, Wahlberg did Robert De Niro's *Raging Bull* in reverse, dropping pounds of muscle to look camera-ready for the slender 1970s. In a neat bookending of body images, Wahlberg's physique first made him the butt of muscle jokes then turned him into a respected actor on every director's A-plus list.

"I lost almost forty pounds to play Dirk," he informed the *New York Times* Syndicate. "When I watched those old porno movies from the 1970s, the thing that struck me the most was that those guys looked so skinny. Maybe those skinny bodies made other things look bigger, or maybe it was all the drugs, booze, and partying. Whatever it was, I wanted that look for Dirk."

Wahlberg kidded about using drugs to slim down for *Boogie Nights*, but immediately made sure everyone knew it was a joke, as reported by the *New York Times* Syndicate. "Being the Method actor that I am, I did coke and all that [laughs]." Mark lost weight the old-fashioned way; he starved himself. "Once I committed, I just starved myself and got myself into being the lean actor they really think I am."

Wahlberg had by now quit cigarettes, but resumed smoking to drop pounds faster.

"So what you see in *Boogie Nights* is less than the old Mark and more, much, much more. I'm going to have to live with Dirk and his diggler for a long time now just as I've had to live with Marky Mark the rapper and Mark the underwear boy," he said.

Actually, Wahlberg had to "live" with Dirk's claim to fame throughout the shoot. Even when he wasn't flashing, the actor had to wear the prop to create what he called the "appropriate bulge" in his pants. "I didn't just wear it for the shock scene. I had to wear it the whole time. It determined the way I had to walk and it provided the appropriate bulge in the costumes."

Like any other "costume," the prosthesis required a fitting in front of lots of production people, including a cameraman. Mark lives with the nightmare that someday photos from this fitting will make their way into the pages of *Playgirl* in a grotesque replay of Brad Pitt's "grimace and bare it" legal battle with the magazine.

"It started the day I got fitted for the penis," he declared for the *New York Times* Syndicate. "There seemed to be dozens of people in the room. Special-effects people, makeup people and wardrobe people. They all insisted they had to take Before and After shots for continuity purposes. I've been assured those photos are never going to be published. Like, yeah. I wasn't born yesterday, but I'm living on hope."

It took half an hour to attach the "prop," and they used glue, Wahlberg claimed. He also joked that the film hired a "penis wrangler" for the messy job of looking after his "costar." Since it took so long to glue on, he wore the little monster all day. "I couldn't pee. I held it all day," he said.

Although he finally said yes to previous no-no's like stripping and singing on film, Wahlberg remained adamant about camera placement, and the director agreed. Mark's face and prosthesis are never seen in the same shot.

In his conversation with Ivor Davis (*New York Times* Syndicate), Mark noted, "I wanted them to cut off my head on-camera for the big unveiling moment. I told Paul that no one was going to be looking at my mug anyway, so why not just show me from the neck down. So that's my body—it's just not my privates."

Just as clothes make the man, *Boogie Nights' Brady Bunch*-style wardrobe also helped him interpret the screen role. "It was just, once you were in, you were in. It was all there. With the clothes and the music—the whole feeling. When you put on those clothes, and you walk, those clothes dictate the way you walk. So it was pretty easy," he said modestly.

CHAPTER 16

Porno-copia

In *Boogie Nights*, as Eddie/Dirk hits bottom, so does most of his dysfunctional porno family, with some falling even faster and lower than Eddie. Amber's cocaine addiction results in the permanent loss of a daughter she adores. Rollergirl descends to "live" pornography in the backseat of a limo, followed by her stomping on the face of her disrespectful costar.

The creepiest fate awaits the Colonel (Robert Ridgely), the self-confident "angel" who bankrolls Horner's films and lives the grand life of a megaproducer in a business whose grosses double the recording industry's ($4 billion vs. $2 billion). Unfortunately, the Colonel also has a night job as a pedophile, and he goes from being a man-about-town with a chauffeured limousine and a tough bodyguard, to a whimpering sex slave physically abused by his cellmate.

In one painful scene, an overweight production assistant, Scotty J. (Philip Seymour Hoffman), finally confesses his unrequited love for Dirk with an open-mouthed kiss and a heartfelt speech that would embarrass a Harlequin romance novelist.

Only Horner remains an anchor amidst all this human flotsam, and even he has crises of the soul. Reynolds' tortured artist laments the transition of porn from film to videotape with the same overwrought anguish with which Norma Desmond assailed the introduction of sound.

But like the true father-figure he has played throughout the film, when Eddie the prodigal surrogate son returns home to Horner and begs to be readmitted to the biz and the "family," he's welcomed back with open arms and a job on a film (oops!—*video*) that is to begin shooting immediately.

The writer-director never lets bathos like that overwhelm his amused take on the subject matter. The "Welcome home, Diggler" scene is immediately followed by Dirk "preparing" himself for a big scene in his comeback project. (Even though he's quit coke, it seems that the effects linger like a bad-acid-trip flashback.) During a motivational monologue in front of a mirror that is both funny for its self-delusion and for its self-importance, Wahlberg's Dirk lectures himself that he is a terrific actor with something "special" indeed.

Finally, after so many rave reviews for his uniqueness, the camera shows exactly what Dirk has to offer: his thirteen-inch penis (a polyurethane stand-in). The final, flaccid image, however, is more ironic than sensationalistic, which may explain why the film earned an R rather than an NC-17 rating. It's obvious Eddie *used to be* special. His claim to fame has fallen on soft times.

Perhaps in a moment of embarrassment regarding the crucial scene, Wahlberg insisted, "I didn't use a stand-in. . . . But it's a trick." He was right about not using another actor as a stand-in, since he delivers a dramatic soliloquy, with full frontal nudity. But as he later admitted to the Associated Press (November 5, 1997), the "main attraction" of the scene was made of plastic, not flesh.

Director Anderson tried to spread a bit of misinformation about the focus of this voyeuristic attention. When asked why he cast Wahlberg in the pivotal role of Diggler, he replied, "He has a thirteen-inch penis so I guess it's typecasting." (In a case of one-upmanship or penis envy, the *Times of London* couldn't resist mentioning that the late John Holmes, whom Dirk's character is loosely based on, had a *fourteen*-inch member of the Screen Actors Guild!)

As the pre-release word-of-mouth became positively garrulous, that Wahlberg had turned in a career-making performance, the actor remained modest about his acting talent. "I just steal everything. I've been really fortunate to work with some amazingly talented people," Mark said.

As their characters do in the film, both Reynolds and Moore took the novice under their wing. Mark generously acknowledged their contribution to making him look so good on-screen: "It made me a lot more comfortable. It was like, 'If I can't look good with these guys, then I might as well just pack up my stuff and go back home.'"

A child of divorce whose father split when Mark was ten, the young man deferred to Reynolds and sought his counsel. Reynolds provided the newcomer with acting tips and life lessons learned the hard way. The older actor served as a role model and cautionary tale whose own past had been almost as checkered as his protégé's. Reynolds' personal problems, including battles with benzodiazapenes and ex-wife Loni Anderson, were arguably more sordid than Wahlberg's. However, their common bonds of public embarrassments and private missteps made them soulmates and helped Mark feel a lot less haunted by his own past.

"The most respected guys out there are those who understand exactly where I came from and what I'm trying to do, especially when dealing with emotions on the screen. Look at Burt Reynolds. He was very familiar with my career ups and downs," Mark explained.

"He has been through the mill more than anyone, from being the world's biggest box-office star to being told he was finished. I heard all the stories about him, too: that he's a maniac, that he's like ice, or an asshole. It's true that he doesn't waste time with people who don't understand him, but he was great to me. He put an arm around my shoulder and gave me some advice. 'Learn to be grateful for all the insults and tough times you've had, because they are going to see you through the next twenty years in this business,' he told me. 'Just don't let the bullshit in Hollywood get to you,'" Mark said to the London *Sunday Times*.

A picture of the two men at the New York premiere of *Boogie Nights* speaks volumes without a single quote in the identifying caption. Mark looks slightly uncomfortable in a jacket and tie. Burt Reynolds, more casually dressed, has his arm around his protégé again, but this time he's not giving him advice, just a squeeze. "Blissful" is an apt term to describe the look on both men's faces.

Shooting the nearly NC-17 sex scenes wasn't blissful, however; it was hard, creepy work that turned the actor *off*, not *on*. Before principal photography began on *Boogie Nights*, Wahlberg worried that he might end up with too much "motivation" because of all the visual stimulation. However, the logistics of filming turned out to be such hard work, he stayed soft. "I feared that I might get turned on in some of the sex scenes," Mark admitted to the London *Sunday Times* in January 1998. "I am standing next to a naked Julianne Moore, pretending to have sex. Julianne is a beautiful woman. So is Heather Graham [Rollergirl]. She lay on top of me, naked—fortunately, there was no sense of arousal. It is true what I have been reading about Hollywood actors who are in love scenes: you're so concerned with lighting, dialogue, and moving in the right way that there's no part of your brain left to think about sex!"

He also kept things from popping up by thinking about costar Moore as a sibling rather than a siren, better than a cold shower for laying low. "I saw Julianne as I would have seen my sister, just the warmest, nicest person in the world. It was not a problem clinging to her. The weird thing was the couple of scenes where we had to portray intimacy—it was awkward. But everybody was just so professional, it was a relief."

Another scene didn't need any body control, except perhaps over the gag reflex. The overweight production assistant, played brilliantly in the story line by Philip Seymour Hoffman, gets drunk and French kisses Dirk. Wahlberg, the alleged homophobe, insisted to *Detour* magazine in May 1997 that he wasn't grossed out and welcomes future acting collaborations with Hoffman.: "I would kiss Phil Hoffman any day of the week, any day," he said, smiling. Although he added, "The only guys I've ever kissed were my brother and Phil. But I'd kiss Phil again anytime because he felt like a brother to me."

While none of Mark's directors has ever accused him of being "difficult" or temperamental, he did find some of the explicit sex scenes in *Boogie Nights* difficult to do and flat-out refused to do them. But not for long. He found director Anderson's gentle cajoling impossible to resist and eventually took a certain exhibitionistic joy, perhaps a holdover from Magic Mountain days, in strutting most of his stuff in front of the camera . . . and supposedly even "around the streets," according to the actor himself.

"There was some quirky porn stuff I just couldn't do and the director was, like, 'Come on, man, this is the best stuff,' and I'm like, 'I just can't, man.'"

Eventually Wahlberg came around to Anderson's voyeuristic point of view. If he could strip down to his Calvins for Klein, he could certainly hang out on the set in swimming trunks. Mark said in the June 1997 issue of *Movieline*, "Coming out wearing nothing but Speedos and cowboy boots was kind of hard. But then it got so I started walking around the streets like that, I was just so into it by that time. It was my ass, literally, so I thought, why not just go for it? This isn't your regular feel-good movie. There's no play for sympathy here like *The People vs. Larry Flynt*. At the end of the day, though, I had to admit to myself, 'Being out there like

Jon Voight in *Midnight Cowboy* is a bag you're going to carry for a long, long time.'"

An associate called *Boogie Nights* a personal exorcism for the actor because his own life paralleled Dirk's in many ways. With no formal training to rely on, Wahlberg delved into his own past to enrich Dirk's present. Asked what the character and the actor had in common, Mark told the *New York Times* Syndicate in early 1998, "I think a lot of things, at different points in my life. I remember when I was at the age where he was at the beginning of the film. I felt the same way, where nobody cared about me, and where I wanted to be liked and loved.... Dirk was a kid with low self-esteem until he became a porn star. I started out a street kid with low esteem until I became a hip-hop artist and a Klein model. That kind of celebrity stuff is like drugs. You don't know what's happening, or why it's happening, but you don't want it to stop. It's too exhilarating. Where I grew up—in the streets of poor Boston—nobody ever told me I was attractive. Suddenly I was on magazine covers, billboards all over the world. It was cool beyond description."

To this day, however, Mark remains perplexed by all the heat he generates. "I still can't understand the whole sex-symbol thing. I look in the mirror and all I see is the pimples on my face."

Wahlberg joked about other similarities between his career and his current alter-ego's: "Neither of us was worried about pulling down our pants. The way I was thrust into the limelight like he was. His search for acceptance. His being away from home, out of the house and looking for love."

All the soul-searching and gooey prop-dangling must have seemed worth the trouble as pre-release buzz about *Boogie Nights* was affirmed by the official tastemakers, movie critics. The reaction in the press seemed more orgasmic than many of the character's best performances. *The New Yorker*'s Daphne Merkin enthused: "I'm almost embarrassed to admit how much I liked *Boogie Nights*, a movie whose male lead is famous for having been a Calvin Klein underwear model. . . ."

Even after a career-making performance, Wahlberg still had to endure snide allusions to his billboard-bimbo incarnation. But not for long. In the same review, Merkin tries to damn the star with faint praise that turns into loud gushing. "Wahlberg plays the part with baffled sweetness; in fact, he's so good at being vulnerable and not too bright that I kept wondering if he was really acting." She adds, "Then again, as people used to say about Brando, this might be great acting."

Like almost every other reviewer, *The New Yorker*'s reserved her greatest praise for the way the film refused to sensationalize, or worse, glamorize a business that basically exists as a marital aid and a lonely onanist's best friend. "*Boogie Nights* has to be the most seductive cautionary tale ever made. Without becoming overtly moralizing, it doesn't shrink from conveying the undertone of Darwinian horror . . . of the porn life."

Sight and Sound conferred the imprimatur of the art-house community by praising the actors, and then singling out Mark for extra kudos. "Sexiness is not [*Boogie Nights*'] foremost pleasure. Performance, however, *is*. The ensemble cast are flawless, although Mark Wahlberg stands out as the well-hung ingénue Eddie."

While the academics and film scholars cooed, the really important voices of the industry, the trade-paper critics, were even chirpier. *Variety* hailed the twenty-seven-year-old director as a "young Scorsese." Its reviewer didn't even take Anderson to task for "borrowing" the opening sequence of Scorsese's *GoodFellas* (1990), one long tracking shot that seems to go on forever—without a single edit or change in camera setup. As Anderson slyly admitted about his homage: "I rip off from the best. The opening shot was done with a Steadicam and we shot it in one night. We rehearsed for three-quarters of the night . . . and did about fourteen takes."

Variety waxed even more boffo about Mark than the film's director had. The trade paper predicted: "Bound to become a star after this movie, Wahlberg renders a splendid performance." *Variety*'s kind words represented more than an ego massage for the actor. No one in the industry reads the reviews in the trades to decide whether or not to check out the movie at the local cineplex. Every mover and shaker in the biz has already seen the film at a private screening on the backlot or the "Bel Air Circuit," a tiny club of top execs, agents, and filmmakers who preview movies at home.

Trade reviews are read because the critics' real job is to be a box-office and career handicapper. The lead in every *Variety* and *Hollywood Reporter* review predicts the commercial prospects of the production and makes sure to comment on each actor's performance. When *Variety* predicted stardom for Wahlberg (a prediction that was more like hindsight after his masterful turn in *Fear*), it wasn't just a pat on the back. It was a major push for his movie career.

Another kind of professional handicapper, a casting director, made a similar prediction about Wahlberg's prospects after seeing *Boogie Nights*: "Where other kids come in all 'actory' and full of poses, he's real, raw, unguarded. Right away, he showed the ambition and the *huevos* [the Anglo agent must have meant *cojones*] to be a real screen presence."

Rolling Stone's Peter Travers, who had hated Mark in *Traveller*, loved him in his follow-up film. "As *Boogie Nights* moves from 1977 to 1984, Wahlberg—with no professional acting training—moves Eddie from sweet child to cynical burnout without a false emotional step."

People magazine expressed the minority view of Mark's performance. But it still couldn't resist using a superlative like "standout": "There are eloquent, energetic performances here by a talented ensemble cast, with the standout being an earnest if dimwitted Wahlberg." *People*'s typically mangled syntax makes it unclear if Eddie/Dirk or the actor himself is dimwitted. If Eddie's the bimbo,

Mark has done his job. If Mark's the moron, his performance isn't a "standout," it's just a stupid guy acting like himself.

To call *Boogie Nights* "transformational" would understate the effect of the film on Wahlberg's career and the industry's perception of him. One interviewer couldn't resist the irony that Mark had to *play* a sex object to get rid of his public image as one. "It would take the role of a sex god to release Wahlberg from the chains of a pumped-up pop icon," Jan Stuart wrote in the *Los Angeles Times* a week after *Boogie Nights'* release.

Perhaps the most exciting "review" came from a non-critic, according to Christopher John Farley, writing in *Time* magazine (October 6, 1997). David Geffen, the mogul who had put a "bug in Calvin Klein's ear" about the youth, predicted, "This new movie of his is going to make him a star. He's built a legitimate career for himself, which he did not have as a recording artist." Geffen had made his original fortune as a record producer, and his brutal honesty about Marky Mark's talent as a rapper gave extra credibility to his praise for Mark Wahlberg, actor. "There's something about Mark, a sexy bad-boy vibe, that's very appealing. People thought he was here today gone tomorrow, but he's going to be here today and here tomorrow," said the billionaire starmaker, who also gave Tom Cruise his big break in *Risky Business* (1983). That kind of prediction from the richest man in Hollywood was even more valuable than *Variety*'s handicapping of his career prospects.

Then there was the respect of others the humble actor would never dare describe as his "peers," although by now that's what they had become. As he pointed out to *Premiere* magazine (May 1998), "The cool people to me, who I would never expect to say nice things—Robert De Niro, Sean Penn, Al Pacino—to come up to me and say, 'Your movie was phenomenal. You were flawless. It was amazing. . . .' To me that is a *huge* deal."

Just as satisfying, however, was a "personal" review from his (unidentified) girlfriend published in the January 11, 1998, issue of the London *Sunday Times*: "I am still in aftershock from the verdict of my girlfriend. She told me, 'I hate to think of you doing all this stuff. It's so *dirty*.' Now she phoned to say it was great and made her laugh. She said to me, 'You look so much bigger onscreen.' I think she meant taller." Praise for the project and even praise for his stature—literally—which a friend has said is the only thing that Wahlberg still feels insecure about.

A review that hadn't come in yet at this time was from a person even closer to the actor than his girlfriend: his mother. Mark was just a bit worried that Alma wouldn't be giggling like his girlfriend or impressed with his on-screen "stature." He predicted, "She's gonna get caught up in the story, but when it's all over, she's gonna say, 'Wow! Did you have to show your ass?'" Eventually Alma turned in her review: "I truly loved it. I think everything that was in the movie needed to be there. . . . I could have lived without the ending."

While *Variety* praised Wahlberg and the film to the skies, it also kept an eye on the bottom line, where its predictions were less stellar. The paper's Emanuel Levy warned that *Boogie Nights*' two-and-a-half-hour length and "risqué subject matter might tarnish box-office results." After that caveat, the reviewer predicted: "No matter how prosperous *Boogie Nights* is at the B.O., it will no doubt establish Anderson as one of the hottest directors of the 1990s."

Boogie Nights reached theaters with lots of baggage. Two recent releases about hard-core sex, *The People vs. Larry Flynt* and *Crash*, had also received terrific reviews, but their box-office take turned out to be anticlimactic. Indeed, the trio of films earned the disapproving sobriquet "raunchfest" from the always tasteful *New York Daily News*.

Variety's crystal ball, as usual, was not clouded. If ever the term *succès d'estime* (i.e., "The critics loved it; the public ignored it!") applied to a movie, *Boogie Nights* merited the moniker.

New Line Cinema released *Boogie Nights* on October 20, 1997, in only two theaters. If the company expected word-of-mouth to spread from such a small platform, it was overly optimistic. Maybe its judgment had been clouded by the reviews. Opening weekend brought in just $50,000 in box-office receipts, a so-so showing. *Boogie Nights* fell off *Variety*'s chart twenty-seven weeks later—the total take, a flaccid $26 million domestic and another $12.8 million abroad.

At least no one could fault the star for failing to promote the film. Wahlberg talked to the *New York Times*, the *Los Angeles Times*, *Time, Newsweek,* and other prestige publications that announced his arrival as a major actor. When chatting with *Out*, which bills itself as "America's Best-Selling Gay and Lesbian Magazine," reporter Peter McQuaid seemed to be covering the teen beat by asking the actor to expose his latest tattoo (the rosary around his neck!). He also asked Mark to describe his dream role (a boxing movie, *Out on My Feet*, a career move that's been put on hold after Robert De Niro fled the project, amid rumors of alleged underworld financing). We also learn from the helpful magazine that Mark doesn't like oral sex—passive or active—and besides, he doesn't have a girlfriend at the moment anyway.

While the Oscars honored costars Julianne Moore, Burt Reynolds, and director Paul Thomas Anderson's screenplay, Wahlberg must have felt like the odd man out when the Academy Award nominations were announced on February 11, 1998.

Amanda Kragten, the Amsterdam-based former head of the international Mark Wahlberg fan club Web site, believes the Oscar snub represented a "Wait and see" attitude by Academy voters. "I think *Boogie Nights* came too early in his career to get a nomination. People still have to get used to the idea that the former Marky Mark actually *can* act! I don't think he's quite ready for an Oscar yet. But in a couple of years with another movie like *Boogie Nights* . . . ," Amanda says hopefully.

Less than a month later, Wahlberg found happier news in the pages of ultra-hip *Details* magazine, which named him "Actor of the Year." Costar Julianne Moore, despite her supporting role, earned Best Actress honors from the same publication. And going where no Oscar nominating committee has ever dared to go, "best sex scene" went to Wahlberg and Moore, although *Details* neglected to mention which one in particular. (While the magazine's editorial board enjoyed several porn-film reenactments that flirted with an NC-17 rating, perhaps the scene that merited *Details'* award was the stars' first close encounter of the lurid kind. Post-orgasm, the cameraman complains that he didn't get "the money shot"—industry jargon for the literally climactic scene where the actor pulls out of the actress and ejaculates. Trouper that he is, Dirk volunteers, "Do you need another take? I can cum again. . . .")

Details also named the production movie of the year, explaining, tongue in cheek, "*Boogie Nights* won the year's top honors with a tale that revealed the truth about growing up in the seventies better than any movie that has come before it except, perhaps, *Halloween*."

Reviews and praise from trendy periodicals consoled Mark and extinguished any self-doubts the film's commercial failure might have caused. The sound of relief is almost audible on the printed page when you read Wahlberg's reaction to the reviews—damn the theater receipts!

"I don't have a problem with people associating me with Marky Mark as far as the music goes," he said from his Hollywood Hills mansion during an interview with the *New York Times,* which took place two months before the film's release because word of mouth was so strong. "But with the whole movie thing, people are not going to see Marky Mark. They're not. Marky Mark is a big part of Mark Wahlberg, but a more trumped-up version. Marky Mark is an energetic, wild kid who pulls his pants down. Mark Wahlberg is grown into a young man." A young man confident enough to refer to himself in the third person.

The same word-of-mouth had inundated him with script offers before *Boogie Nights'* release. Career-clever as usual, he was doing a lot of looking before he leaped into his next venture. He remained self-possessed enough to keep at arm's length the young man who had made his career, *Boogie Nights* director Paul Thomas Anderson, when he asked Mark to star in a new, tailor-made script he had written. And with the same self-confidence, he could say no to other entreaties from even bigger names.

In fact, he set his sights very high, the mountaintop actually, when he used a magazine interview to solicit work from the man whom many consider *the* greatest director currently working in the film industry. *Boogie Nights* might have imitated the opening scene of *GoodFellas*. But now Wahlberg felt worthy enough to "speak" directly to the director of the real thing during a chat with *Movieline* magazine. "After *Boogie Nights*, it's hard for me to watch anything or want to commit to anything that isn't really wild. I'd really love to work with Martin Scorsese. Those are the movies that I really love.

"Marty, better give me a call soon . . . !"

The same self-confidence that had him pursuing screenwork with the director of *Raging Bull* also allowed Mark to finally embrace his past concert and billboard exposures as essentially good career moves. In hindsight, Wahlberg felt *he* had used his body rather than being used by Klein and fans.

The same month *Boogie Nights* was released, he was asked if he regretted "doing the stud thing" for the Calvin Klein underwear campaign.

"God, no," he told the media, "'cause I've been acting. Because if I was never really a stud, I never would have gotten an opportunity to act. . . . It wasn't like the tag on the back of jeans where the body's there and they cut the head off," Mark said. "There was still a lot being said through me and my face and my eyes. It wasn't the worst thing, but it wasn't the best. Like all the other things I did, it was fun while it lasted."

Compare that happy thought post-*Boogie Nights* with the anxiety he had expressed only a few years earlier, that his spur-of-the-moment decision to drop his pants at Magic Mountain had turned into a regular feature of his stage act because fans demanded it.

His flashy, fleshy past behind him, Mark liked his new "location." "I'm in a place now where people are judging my work, and not me."

But even more important, as *Boogie Nights* came out and flopped, Wahlberg was literally in a different place, once again far away on location, making *The Big Hit* in Toronto.

Distance from Hollywood and its microscopic handicapping of his career prospects didn't provide the only analgesic. A box-office flop can seriously brutalize a star's bank account. The embarrassing gross doesn't just hurt his or her ego, it can also reduce his or her asking price for future screen assignments. Wahlberg wasn't making any frantic calls to his business manager, however, when he scanned the charts and saw *Boogie Nights* sliding down them.

Although New Line Cinema paid him the coolie wage of $150,000 for that film ("not enough to cover expenses," one magazine said, of his expensive entourage), *The Big Hit* was a big film from Sony, the biggest studio conglomerate. And this time, Mark's payday was very rewarding.

While the star's handlers refused to reveal his exact fee for the movie, a mutual friend told me Wahlberg collected $1.9 million for *The Big Hit*, an action flick that Wahlberg hoped would propel him into the stratosphere of action stars like Bruce Willis and Arnold Schwarzenegger. With *Boogie Nights*, he had paid his dues and become heir apparent to Robert De Niro. He even had had the chutzpah to offer his services to De Niro's "De Niro" in the directing field, *GoodFellas*' Martin Scorsese. With *The Big Hit* and a follow-up cop caper, *The Corruptor* (1999), Wahlberg hoped he might join Tom Cruise and Harrison Ford in the box-office big league.

CHAPTER 17

Marquee Mark Hits It Big

If I can continue to do good movies, then I could be very happy. I could hang up the underwear.

—Mark Wahlberg, 1998

Friends say Wahlberg is the least materialistic person they know. Despite an early flirtation with shopaholism and a $100,000 Mercedes, "stuff" doesn't mean anything to the actor, as evidenced by the minimal furnishings of his West Hollywood penthouse.

The Big Hit really wasn't about making a couple of million dollars. It wasn't even about starring in a movie with a possible $200 million gross that would give him the clout to name his next projects and directors. Bruce Willis has often said he makes all those *Die Hard* movies to pay the bills while he takes intriguing supporting roles in quirky films like *Nobody's Fool* (1994) and *North* (1994—as the Easter Bunny!) that pay Guild-minimum peanuts. If *The Big Hit*, an action caper, did *Die Hard*-type business, Wahlberg could conceivably undertake a pet project, his fantasy equivalent of Mel Gibson's *Braveheart* (1995), Kevin Costner's *Dances with Wolves* (1990), or Robert Redford's *Ordinary People* (1980), which turned mere screen-studs into Oscar-winning stud-directors. A blockbuster movie would indeed let Wahlberg utter the D-word. ("I want to direct!")

Nevertheless, friends say Mark didn't sign on for money *or* clout when he agreed to make *The Big Hit*. He wanted to stretch as an actor. He also wanted to banish his lingering obsession that people still saw him as that guy in jockey shorts on a Times Square billboard. Indeed, a huge financial success would allow him to banish once and for all his image as a male lingerie model. "That's all I want to do," he said to the press about expanding his range on the Toronto set of *The Big Hit*. "If I can continue to do good movies, then I could be very happy. I could hang up the underwear."

Most people, of course, had already forgotten about his Calvin Klein modeling past, but a tiny bit of insecurity still made the actor self-conscious about his claim to infamy. As he said just a bit defensively about his body, "I have it so I use it. I think my body helped my career only because there's a lot on the inside, there's a lot upstairs." Mark was stating the obvious: If all it took was a great bod, Fabio, not Kevin Kline, would be performing Chekhov on Broadway.

The Big Hit was a gangster (that's gangster, not *gangsta*!) caper. Early pre-production news stories about the plot made it seem as though Mark was retreading stale waters—only with a much bigger budget. If he really wanted to stretch, why was he doing an action film, where typically the cars, not the characters, get more screen attention? The announcements in the trades didn't help the misperception about the movie's subject matter.

According to one industry publication, *The Big Hit* would star Mark as a hit man who makes a big mistake. He kidnaps the goddaughter of a mob boss. The director, Hong Kong chopsockey auteur Che-Kirk Wong, was being imported to the United States, actually Canada, by TriStar Pictures with another martial-arts director who made the transition to mainstream movies, John Woo (*Face/Off*, 1997), as executive producer.

Wesley Snipes, an action star, owned the rights to the script, and Snipes' production company had brought the project to TriStar. Interestingly, Snipes, too, was trying to shed his Uzi-armed image and did not appear in the feature, except in the credits.

Only one trade story bothered to mention that *The Big Hit* was an action *comedy*. Pre-release, it took a laborious combing of cyberspace to find out, from the keyboard of the scriptwriter himself, that *The Big Hit* was actually a romantic comedy set in the crime world. Somehow screenwriter Ben Ramsey had logged on and accessed the Marky Mark fan club Web site. Ramsey found himself fielding questions from other onliners who sounded like fans—twelve-year-old fans.

Ramsey reported online that Wahlberg played Melvin Smiley, a hit man who's ripped off by his mistress (Lela Rochon) and engaged to a Jewish-American princess from hell (Christina Applegate). However, the hit man hits it off with and falls for his kidnap victim, played by fashion model China Chow, daughter of celebrity restaurateur, Michael ("Mr.") Chow.

Comic relief from all this heavy breathing comes from the fact that Wahlberg's dimbulb character kidnaps Chow without knowing she's the Godfather's goddaughter. The action plays second fiddle to the action scenes with Wahlberg, Chow, Rochon, and Applegate (of TV's *Married......With Children*). If Wahlberg wanted to sharpen his chops as a romantic leading man, who better than with Applegate, a TV version of Marilyn Monroe?

And that's exactly why Mark picked *The Big Hit* out of all the movie scripts that were offered him after *Boogie Nights*. He had played a psychotic lover in *Fear* and an impotent lover in *Boogie Nights*. *The Big Hit*, under cover of a bankable action movie, represented his chance to invade the celluloid world of romantic comedy. Screenwriter Ramsey called Mark's Mevin Smiley the "Michael Jackson" of hit men: professionally, a sex symbol; personally, "a mess," Ramsey said of his screen creation.

Applegate wants to marry Mark, but her motivation isn't romantic. She's engaged to the hit man to annoy her uptight parents. He's also floated a huge cash loan for his would-be in-laws. Dad (Elliott Gould) is addicted to booze; mom (Lainie Kazan) is addicted to gambling and plastic surgery.

If Wahlberg wanted to play a ladies' man on-camera, he has three chances in this project. Besides his fiancée and abductee, he also has a beautiful African-American mistress. "Date movies" are usually picked by the female half of the date, and the casting of black, Asian, and Caucasian women suggests the studio was trying to cover all the demographic bases. As if Mark's Smiley doesn't have enough problems with his Jewish bride and Chinese infatuation, Rochon's character constantly demands huge amounts of money from Mark's "hero" for car and mortgage payments. Plus, she has a bodybuilder boyfriend to support!

Sony, which owns TriStar, hedged its bets in bankrolling the romantic comedy by making sure there were enough gun battles *if* Mark failed to deliver as a romantic leading man. Or as scriptwriter Ramsey phrased it in cyberspace fast-chat: "Mark shoots lots of guns and eventually prevails over everyone who is stepping on him. *The Big Hit* is an Action/Comedy kind of like *Pulp Fiction* or *Reservoir Dogs* only with a real good looking cast."

Indeed, the casting folks at Sony/TriStar added another stud to the movie lineup to make sure teenage girls didn't miss opening weekend at the multiplex. If Wahlberg supplied one type of fantasy image, Antonio Sabato Jr. would bring in another adoring segment, as the main man's colleague-in-crime.

Wahlberg must have enjoyed the irony of working with Sabato, tinged with a bit of relief that his own career wasn't where Sabato's was at the moment—hunk in transition. While they worked together on the set of *The Big Hit* in the summer of 1997, Sabato was also appearing elsewhere. He was on billboards across the country, clad only in underwear, displaying the same Calvin Klein logo around his waist that Mark had come to dread.

Wahlberg fanciers, however, couldn't help but point out snidely that while Antonio had the face of a Caravaggio, his muscles didn't come close to Wahlberg's perfection.

Wahlberg, of course, would never have made such an invidious comparison between the stars' bods. As usual, he was charming to every single co-worker, including screenwriter Ramsey. His kindness toward a writer with no real clout was, of course, reflexive, but then again, you never know. Today's obscure screenwriter may turn into tomorrow's A-list director.

Whatever his motivation, Wahlberg did more than sign an autograph for Ramsey's mother at the screenwriter's request. Ramsey said in cyberia, "I also got to meet Mark and the cast. I must say that Mark is the greatest. A real gentleman, he is equal parts cool and friendly and he gave my mother a nice video greeting. I guess you can say I'm a new fan now." And Mom has her own personalized Marky Mark video.

In case all the teen demographic bases hadn't been covered—or smothered—by now, *The Big Hit*'s multiculturalism targeted the Native American/Pacific Islander/Asian audience with Lou Diamond Phillips in a supporting role as a hit man who brings his work home with him; i.e., he kills his partners.

With *The Big Hit*, Wahlberg was turning into the De Niro of his generation in more ways than one. Not only an excellent actor and heir to the Method, he was beginning to use his body like plastic in the Greek sense of the word: moldable. (Or maybe it was an eating disorder.) Whatever his motivation, Method or madness, Wahlberg, already thirty pounds lighter from his incarnation as a scrawny 1970s porn star, dropped more weight for *The Big Hit*.

"I've got some scoops," a Web-site scanner who only gave her name as Faiza breathlessly typed on the Marky Mark site. "My friend ended up as an extra for the movie and she almost didn't recognize Mark because he has gotten so skinny! She said his muscles are gone!" Faiza reported the transformation with a real sense of loss and perhaps frustrated lust.

Another extra rushed to Wahlberg's defense on Mark's site, insisting, "We met Mark on July 28 in Toronto on the set. He did NOT look 'skinny' to us. He was very nice and we got photos. His hair is colored a strawberry blond and he still looks FINE as ever!"

The truth of Mark's physical transformation lay somewhere in between the two conflicting fan reports. Early in *The Big Hit*, there's a scene showing a shirtless (surprise!) Mark practicing martial arts and an obvious stunt double using a pommel horse. Wahlberg's bod was no longer poster-perfect. "Lean and hard" rather than "skinny" best describes the famous torso.

On nights and days off from shooting in Toronto, Wahlberg didn't do the movie-star trip. He holed up in his hotel or Winnebago between camera setups. Fans spotted him dining out at such untrendy spots as McDonald's, which doesn't explain the weight loss. At the Toronto Film Festival, which took place during the shoot, Wahlberg and costar Lou Diamond Phillips turned up for the premiere of Brad Pitt's film *Seven Years in Tibet*.

At the movie party afterward, one gala goer said, "I had the pleasure of meeting both of them. Mark is a total sweetheart and cute as ever! He was taking time to speak to everyone and was goofing around with Lou [Diamond Phillips]. Mark is definitely one of the good ones!"

The Big Hit's summer shoot ran into the fall, and the production was still in Toronto when *Boogie Nights* premiered there on September 12, 1997. As if the film crew and its cast of ensemble studs and bombshells hadn't created enough interest, the glitzy premiere of the most controversial film of the year added fuel to the inflamed curiosity.

Fans blocked Mark's entrance to the movie theater until he signed autographs, which he did, typically, without complaint. In fact, one happy recipient said, "He stopped to sign a few autographs and talked to anyone who would talk to him." Two other signature hounds, Leslie and Laura, said, "We never knew that one man could look so hot in a suit!! Heat wave in Toronto!"

After the screening, Wahlberg, the director, and costars appeared onstage for a Q&A, although the topics discussed went unrecorded for posterity—at least, not on the Web site devoted to *The Big Hit* and its main star.

To publicize *Boogie Nights* at the Toronto Film Festival and give it a promotional push as it made its way south of the border, Wahlberg took time out from the demands of filming *The Big Hit* and made personal appearances at two festival screenings of *Boogie Nights*.

Post-premiere, Wahlberg joined the cast at the nightclub Babalu, but by now he had had enough of fan frenzy and asked to be left alone. Ignoring his day job as role model, Wahlberg puffed on cigars and knocked back beers. A partygoer described the star as "mellow," despite his standoffishness.

Back at work on the set after all the parties and promotions, Wahlberg must have felt it was déjà vu all over again. *Boogie Nights* featured several scenes where he had to simulate masturbation (or attempt it). In *The Big Hit*, Wahlberg has a similar scene with a fellow hitman with a taste for porn movies and self-gratification. "I was practicing lines with one of the cast members, in prep for filming and was so embarrassed about the beginning part when Mark talks about jerking off!! It made me blush!!" This revelation from an extra on the set hit the Internet a week before the Toronto premiere of *Boogie Nights*. You wonder what color the extra turned when she saw Mark do more than discuss self-stimulation in *Boogie Nights'* climactic scene.

The Big Hit came in at only $10 million, much less than the $40 million average budget for a Hollywood film nowadays. The relatively small budget suggests Sony/TriStar may have been further hedging its bets with the still-unproven Wahlberg and hadn't heard the booming word-of-mouth on the as-yet-unreleased *Boogie Nights.*

As an example of just what small change $10 million was for a stunts-and-squealing-tires epic like *The Big Hit*, in the same trade story announcing that Hong Kong director John Woo would produce *The Big Hit*, the paper mentioned that Woo was also directing *Face/Off*. That film, which would turn into a sleeper and critical hit later that summer, boasted a budget of $90 million! However, it had the services of John Travolta and Nicolas Cage, both hot after scorching hits like *Pulp Fiction* (1994) and *Con Air* (1997).

Studios would feel the box-office heat after *Boogie Nights* came out on October 20, 1997. After highly positive reviews for Mark and the movie, no studio would offer the newly minted star a tepid $10 million action film. New Line Cinema, seeking to shed its art-house image with a blockbuster release, would offer Wahlberg $2.5 million for his screen services on *The Corruptor* (1999), an action film it hoped would do *Die Hard* business. Not by coincidence, the offer from New Line was announced two weeks *after Boogie Nights* was released. The mere fact that Mark was considering making the picture merited the front-page attention of the *Hollywood Reporter*, which revealed, "Wahlberg has been the center of fierce attention in recent weeks as he has gained heat off his performance in New Line's *Boogie Nights*."

Other projects, dutifully reported as major headline news—at least in the trades—swarmed around the new superstar. Universal hoped he would star in *The Green Hornet.* Micromanager Mark summarily rejected it as too crass for the career he was brilliantly building. To recapture the services of the star of the studio's *Fear*, Universal offered the actor $10 million to play the title role of the crusading do-gooder in a big-budget screen adaptation of the 1960s TV crime drama. It was, at best, a questionable project, since the half-hour series had lasted less than one season in 1966. Again, the actor kept his gaze way above the bottom line and sought to stretch his acting abilities, not his bank account. *Green Hornet* was vetoed by the increasingly self-confident young man.

At the opposite end of the taste spectrum, Wahlberg had already reported to the set of *Out on My Feet* because Robert De Niro was also there, ready to costar. (The demise of that movie project will be examined in a later chapter.)

Columbia, another member of the Sony movie studio family, crazily wooed the skin flick star with an offer of yet another skin flick, *8mm*, but by now Wahlberg had had enough of flexposure.

When *The Big Hit* hit number one at the box office its opening weekend, April 24, 1998, TriStar must have been delighted it had paid almost $2 million for the star's service (according to reports in the trades).

In 2,149 theaters, *The Big Hit* grossed $10.8 million during the first three days of its release, stomped two hit romantic comedies (*City of Angels* and *Object of My Affection*), and swamped the billion-dollar, long-running *Titanic,* which sank to fourth place in the wake of the Wahlberg juggernaut.

The film's business was even more spectacular considering the lukewarm promotion the studio had put behind *The Big Hit*: Minimal TV spots. Less than full-paged newspaper ads. And the distribution date itself, as a post-Easter, pre-summer blockbuster release, suggested the studio was dumping the picture. Tom Cruise movies *do not* open in late April when the kids are still in school. And spring break, a big time for moviegoing, ended weeks before *The Big Hit* reached theaters. The critic for the *New York Times*, which usually leaves box-office predictions to the professional soothsayers at the trades, mentioned that the studio had dumped the film. In fact, reviewer Lawrence Van Gelder said the following in the lead of what was supposed to be a movie review, not a commentary on studio politics: "If *The Big Hit* had any valid claim to excellence, rest assured that its release would have been delayed till summer."

The reviews must have also scared the studio before the weekend box-office proved that *The Big Hit* was critic-proof, like Jim Carrey movies.

Daily Variety's Leonard Klady said, "Despite the thinness of the amusing material, the cast manages to elevate the piece several notches. Wahlberg's hangdog look and pained expression is perfectly employed for wry comic effect. His character's inkling of self-awareness makes him the type of existential [!?] hero who's unusual for the genre."

The *Hollywood Reporter*'s Michael Rechtshaffen wrote, "With female-driven date movies crowding the box office, there's ample opportunity for *The Big Hit* to become at least a moderate hit for TriStar." The critic, however, didn't show any doubts about the star's performance. "Wahlberg delivers a pitch-perfect, comically straight performance."

Perhaps the most sulfurous review came from Los Angeles-based *Entertainment Today*. "Utterly ridiculous from beginning to end, *The Big Hit* is the type of film that straddles the precipice between a straightforward action film and gross parody. This . . . makes for ninety-some minutes of cinematic hell."

However, the *Entertainment Today* critic praised the "hellish" film's star: "Mark Wahlberg . . . is the best thing about this turkey. . . . He not only proves himself a viable action hero, but is possessed of enough charisma to claim the lion's share of *The Big Hit*'s scarce bearable moments. . . . Wahlberg somehow wades through this mess unscathed." Typically, even when a critic hated a Wahlberg film, he liked Mark's performance very much.

Reviewers always seemed to love it when Wahlberg stretched creatively. These days Mark was willing to tackle almost anything except iambic pentameter. "I want to stay away from Shakespeare," he said in 1998.

The *Los Angeles Times'* Jack Matthews complained that *The Big Hit* rolled too many genres into one big mess in an attempt to target so many demographics. "*The Big Hit* is that rarest of all genre hybrids, the screwball-romantic-action-situation-black comedy. Rare for good reason. Who'd want to see a thing like that? The gamble here is that kids will"—although Matthews was not optimistic. "*The Big Hit* is nothing more or less than a big goof." And the only praise the usually generous Matthews offered Wahlberg was to describe his hitman as an "amiable antihero."

The *New York Times*' critic offered consumer tips to would-be theatergoers. "Insatiable moviegoers are advised to wait till this action-comedy . . . thuds into video stores; tasteful moviegoers will avoid it altogether." Still, the *Times* found time to praise the star. "In the preposterous plot, Wahlberg manages to elicit sympathy for his portrayal of Mel, a neurotic young hit man."

Indeed, Wahlberg's sociopath in the film is more than just neurotic; as his college-educated kidnap victim (Chow) points out, he's dysfunctional, a classic codependent! Or, as Mark's Mel Smiley says several times in the film, "I can't stand the idea of nobody liking me!"

While critics complained that *The Big Hit* was a stale combination of various movie genres, the concept of a codependent contract killer was fresh, even unique. Sitting in his penthouse, reading scripts, Mark must have recognized the originality of Mel's conflicted character, a hit man with a heart of gold. If *The Big Hit* proved anything, it was that Wahlberg had translated his street-smarts into script-smarts—the ability to read a screenplay and figure out if it will make money. Tom Cruise has this same script-reading talent.

Although it was his first English-language film, Hong Kong director Che-Kirk Wong managed to juggle witty dialogue with scenes of barbarity. The director and the screenwriter make the audience hurl and howl at the same time in a scene where Mark washes off chopped-up body parts of a victim in the bathtub while his mistress, oblivious to what he's doing, complains about late payments on her Mercedes and the mortgage. And while he's scouring the odd foot in the tub or shooting a college student in cold blood, Mark maintains our sympathy for the codependent Mel, a major acting feat in itself.

Followers of Wahlberg's screen evolution will notice the actor's clout in limiting the amount of skin exposure—at least his own. In not one but two repetitious locker room scenes, the hit men display everything, including buns, stopping short of the full monty. Everyone, that is, except Mark, whose back remains all that we see in the locker room. It was Wahlberg's decision to butt out of these scenes. "I told Kirk [the director], if you want me to, I will, but I just kind of did it [in *Boogie Nights*]." And Donnie wasn't there to change his mind or pull his brother's pants down. Mark's career didn't need that kind of exposure at this point.

In interviews, the actor has admitted he worries about his physique, although he willingly trashes it for the good of a role. You wonder how he felt watching the dailies of these nude scenes. Antonio Sabato Jr., standing near his Klein colleague, dwarfs the star. And Sabato's body looks much more muscular than the one on display in Calvin Klein ads and billboards, more pumped even than Mark's was during his stint as an underwear spokestud.

If Wahlberg chose *The Big Hit* to show he could do romantic comedy, he succeeded very well indeed. The kosher-chicken-stuffing scene with China Chow is the funniest substitute sex act since Albert Finney and a chippie munched on a drumstick in *Tom Jones* (1963). In *The Big Hit* Mark is also saddled with the near impossible task of making his kidnap victim, whom he physically abuses, fall in love with him. It was a tough task, but Wahlberg did it successfully on-camera.

A Spanish proverb says revenge is a dish best served cold. Wahlberg eventually got his gazpacho, chillin' till he was hot enough to take on the Material Girl one more time after their rumble in the Hollywood Hills.

In 1993, when Mark was still a struggling actor, he may have regretted comparing Madonna to a rotten, rotting demon like Beetlejuice. At the time, it wasn't a good career move to tick off a major star. A few years later, as Madonna's film career seemed more and more like a sad joke, and Mark had become a major movie star, he may have felt empowered enough to make an even stronger criticism of a woman who almost killed his career by claiming he was homophobic.

"I have the utmost respect for Madonna, but that's changing," he told Erik Hedegaard in the April 1996 issue of *Details* magazine. "She's out there dissing Mariah Carey. That's someone she can't even stand next to. Come on! Better take your ass back to that karaoke bar. Don't ever put a microphone in her hand. It's like going out there and selling crack or heroin. Everybody might be buying it, but that don't mean it's good. My feeling is, don't try to fool yourself. You're not only going to suffer and find yourself pretty damn miserable. Can't fight the truth, bro."

CHAPTER 18

Simply Incorruptible

Friends and colleagues have already established Mark Wahlberg was not out to make a quick buck. A wannabe Harrison Ford doesn't make a *no*-budget independent film like *Traveller* after a major-studio film like *Fear*. The script and what it could do for his career, not the bottom line, got the actor's attention. *The Big Hit*, he hoped, would add a different kind of role to his acting résumé.

The decision to sign on for *The Corruptor* (1999) suggested career management rather than artistic considerations was the deciding factor. Whereas *The Big Hit* navigated new career waters for Mark, *The Corruptor* was pure Hollywood popcorn, date-night moviemaking at its most commercial and calculated.

The Corruptor is the true story of a Chinese cop in Chinatown. A good cop gone bad, the detective finds his compulsive gambling leads to blackmail by his creditor, the head of a Triad gang, called the Manipulator.

In an unusual bit of reverse casting, the Chinese cop gets a white partner. The usual pecking order in casting a cop-buddy picture goes like this: white movie star teams with B-list black actor. The poor black cop is usually weeks away from retirement when he bites the bullet, sending his aggrieved white partner into ballistic Bronson mode. (One critic called it "Mel Gibson-Danny Glover syndrome." Warner Bros. called it a franchise that has so far grossed half a billion dollars with endless sequels to hold up the tent poles on the back lot in Burbank.)

The white partner in *The Corruptor*, of course, is Mark Wahlberg. The package had lots of what is called "synergy"—the impressive parts made an even more terrific sum. Wahlberg must have felt as though he were returning home when he signed on with New Line Cinema, the company that had given him his first dramatic break in *The Basketball Diaries*, then bestowed stardom with its *Boogie Nights*. Wahlberg was grateful, but so was the mini-major studio, and showed *its* gratitude with a $2.5 million payday for the boy from Boston.

A bigger gamble was handing over the lead to an actor with the unintentionally funny name of Chow Yun-Fat. No one was laughing at New Line Cinema, however, because although Fat might sound like the butt of a Joan Rivers Roseanne/Liz Taylor joke, Fat was the number one box-office star of Hong Kong's superlucrative chopsockey epics. One colleague said of the friendly Fat, "He's like Steven Seagal, but with charisma." Actually, Fat's box office was fatter than Seagal's by now.

Wahlberg also felt at home with the man at the helm of *The Corruptor*, James Foley, who had transformed the callow rap star into a studly psycho in their previous collaboration, *Fear*. Ironically, where Foley had earlier presented languid shots of Wahlberg unclothed in bed with a mostly clothed female star, in *The Corruptor*, both director and star collaborated in the "spoiling" of Wahlberg's body.

To play a New York City detective who spends more time at donut shops than at World's Gym across from Lincoln Center,

Wahlberg ballooned up to 200 pounds. That's why he was unrecognizable and looked like a young Orson Welles when I saw him working out at Gold's in early 1998. Wahlberg had gone to fat, but this time his career, not the love of junk food, was the reason for his weight gain.

Just as he had trashed his body-beautiful image to near anorexia for *Boogie Nights*, the supremely unvain actor was willing—temporarily—to be the butt of fat jokes and snickers behind his back at the gym.

James Foley, the director, said he wanted Mark to weigh 200 pounds for the role of an internal-affairs detective, and Mark is famous for taking "direction." In fact, the conscientious star went about adding the weight so efficiently the director was shocked when he saw the effects of his request.

"Jamie came to see me and freaked out. People from the studio heard, and someone called and wanted to know my weight," Wahlberg said. Eventually, he "slimmed" down to 185, his current poundage, which is still pretty hefty compared to his billboard days when he was a lean, mean 150 pounds. To gain the original poundage, Mark quit smoking. He may have had a hard time losing it because he went back to smoking post-production. A visitor in his New York hotel suite suggested he might be a chain-smoker, describing an ashtray as "crowded with American Spirit butts."

Whatever physical humiliation he underwent for *The Corruptor,* it was worth it. While director Foley was still proving his screen status, there was A-plus Oscar talent behind the camera in the form of executive producer Oliver Stone. Even if the film flopped, Wahlberg would be able to pick up the phone and have Stone take his call when the director who made Tom Cruise a serious Oscar contender in *Born on the Fourth of July* (1989) was casting his future film projects. If Wahlberg behaved himself, which he always did, Stone would at the very least be willing to consider him for a classier production than a genre film like *The Corruptor*.

Indeed, *The Corruptor*'s director, who didn't need any convincing, revealed that Stone pushed him to hire Wahlberg. "Oliver Stone . . . said, 'We have to get Mark to do this movie because he's just somebody that you really want to sit and look at.' I thought that really summed up what makes a movie star. There are so many people I don't want to sit there and look at!" Foley admitted.

Press reports about *The Corruptor* during pre-production suggest how far up the food chain Wahlberg had climbed since *Boogie Nights*. The mere fact that he was "attached" to a project, as the trades said about *The Corruptor*, made headlines in the industry press and gave whatever project he was involved in instant credibility. He was possibly only one megahit away from superstar status, also known as bankability. His name "attached" to a production would secure instant financing. Only a handful of stars are bankable today, and even they have relatively short shelf-lives with the fickle public.

While *The Corruptor* provided the added sweetener of letting Mark hang with Oliver Stone, he turned down the supplications of an even hotter director, Joel Schumacher, who specializes in turning young studs into stud-superstars. (See George Clooney, Val Kilmer, and Chris O'Donnell for examples of the Schumacher magic.)

Unfortunately, Schumacher's baby, *8mm* (1999), seemed like Frankenstein's monster to Wahlberg. The subject matter of *8mm* would have plunged him farther into the world of porn. A quick dip in the fetid waters of hard-core filmmaking did wonders for his career with *Boogie Nights*, but *8mm* would have taken him where no legit actor has ever dared to go.

Even so, *8mm*'s pedigree must have been tempting. Not only did it have *Batman*'s billion-dollar director aboard, but Kevin Walker, who wrote the ultra-sleek, ultra-sick *Se7en* (1995), penned the script. The subject matter needed the services of a writer who could make a head in a FedEx box the MacGuffin in a Brad Pitt film. The subject matter also had to be a major turnoff for

Wahlberg, especially after one trip to the X-rated film world—only, *8mm*'s universe represented an even creepier milieu, snuff films. For the uninitiated, snuff films are beyond XXX-rated; the star, usually a woman, literally dies at the end. Forget about clever puns that the end is climactic in more ways than one. For the necrophiliac pleasures of their viewers, snuff films off the leading lady. The producers are obviously not Screen Actors Guild signatories.

Snuff films are pure fantasy. Researchers—not to mention the police—have tried in vain to find a real-life (if that's the right word for such a lethal medium) snuff film, and they always come up empty-handed. South America is usually the alleged source of such movies, but no one has ever located one outside the busy rumor mill, a nightmarish version of Hollywood's dream factory.

Joaquin Phoenix, who played the impressionable teen sociopath in *To Die For* (1995), stepped in to take the role rejected by Wahlberg. *8mm,* which Wahlberg turned down and Phoenix perhaps not so wisely accepted, is about a seedy private eye who is hired by a woman to find out the origin of a snuff film found in her dead husband's safety-deposit box. Wahlberg would have played yet another porn star, who serves as the tour guide for the detective's descent into films rated X for "X-ecution."

Even if *8mm* hadn't been a more grotesque revisiting of terrain Wahlberg already explored in *Boogie Nights*, he would have had to pass on the project, which was set to begin production in June 1998. June was also the start date of Wahlberg's next project, *The Yards*. By now, the actor was turning into a workaholic. He had made two films, *Boogie Nights* and *The Big Hit*, in 1997. Then two more films back-to-back in 1998. *The Corruptor* started shooting in March and as soon as it wrapped, he had to report to the set of *The Yards* (1999), a crime drama about the murder of a New York City transit cop.

The Yards was another smart career move for Wahlberg. *The Big Hit* was a crime comedy that would also serve as a vehicle for Wahlberg's trip to romantic-leading-man land. *The Corruptor* was a no-brainer cop movie that could become a blockbuster and grant him bankability to play anything he wanted to on-screen.

The Yards combined the best of both ingredients for a viable acting career, crass and class. With class alone, you get Meryl Streep, brilliant and underemployed after one too many succès d'estime. Crass creates Jim Carrey and Tim Allen, constantly employed but usually with as much respect as Rodney Dangerfield gets.

The Corruptor's studio, New Line Cinema, may have been the Tiffany's of independents, but *The Yards* was being bankrolled by the Fort Knox of major-minis, Miramax Films. Although owned by Disney, Miramax these days seems to be Oscar's home away from home, with Academy Award winners like *The English Patient* (1996) and *Good Will Hunting* (1997). Wahlberg didn't get Oscar recognition for *Boogie Nights*, but with Miramax's pedigree and promotional push, he might be showing up at the Shrine in 2000 for *The Yards*.

Miramax's kingmaker, Harvey Weinstein, promised that the mini-studio would be behind this Wahlberg project all the way: "*The Yards* has been a labor of love for Miramax, and I am very excited to be able to announce a cast of this caliber," he said. The script by James Gray and Matt Reeves wasn't too shabby, either, and Weinstein compared it to *Chinatown* (1974) and *The Godfather* (1972).

The comparison to the screen classics was not all hype. *The Yards* revolves around a WASP crime family, headed by James Caan, who owns a company that services and supplies parts for the New York transit system. Wahlberg and Joaquin Phoenix play best friends who get sucked into the family's corrupt business practices.

The film had so much heat behind it—plus Disney's checkbook—that instead of shooting in the cheaper, urban-generic Toronto, Miramax forked over the funds to make it in ultra-expensive New York City.

Once again, Wahlberg may have felt uncomfortable exploring semi-autobiographical plot elements like a just-released con who unwittingly gets involved in the murder of a police officer. His costar, Joaquin Phoenix, River's younger brother, was a future star in the making after holding his own against Nicole Kidman in *To Die For*.

Veteran actor James Caan would provide ballast for the young cast. Caan's career has had as many ups and downs as a roller-coaster ride. Caan also has a reputation for experiencing the ancient industry euphemism "creative differences" with costars and directors. In recent years, an apt analogy for his career might be "on the down escalator." By signing on to *The Yards*, he may have hoped to attach his falling star to Wahlberg's ascendant one.

Industry observers weren't predicting any star feuds on *The Yards,* since Wahlberg is famous for deferring to older costars, having charmed the likes of Burt Reynolds and Danny DeVito. Wahlberg might give attitude to a colleague close to his age, like *Boogie Nights'* Paul Thomas Anderson, but even interviewers older than the young star comment on his habit of addressing them as "sir" or "ma'am."

Besides being an important transition in Wahlberg's movie career since *The Yards* combines commercial potential with a character study, the movie represents classic packaging where an outside agency, rather than the studio or even the filmmakers, creates the "package" or the elements of a project. *The Yards'* director, James Gray, and cast members Wahlberg, Caan, Phoenix, and Charlize Theron were all repped by United Talent Agency, *the* hottest firm in the business. Film lovers have long complained about agents instead of filmmakers serving as casting directors, but when you have a powerful stable of clients working in front of and behind the camera, clout equals taste.

For most of 1998, Wahlberg immersed himself in back-to-back filmmaking. The busy schedule, besides burnishing his career and résumé, may have kept his mind off the career-making project that got away, *Out on My Feet*. Work also helped him forget about the kingmaker, Robert De Niro, who fled the ultimate fantasy project for a young actor seeking A-list status (A as in *art*) rather than B-list muscle (B as in *box office*).

Freezing in Toronto and chilling in New York City on first *The Corruptor* and then *The Yards,* helped take the heat off losing a chance to work with every young actor's idol and role model—the screen's Raging Bull himself.

CHAPTER 19

Requiem for a Cruiserweight

If ever there was a dream project for an up-and-coming actor with ambition to burn and learn, *Out on My Feet* had to be that project. In October 1997, *Boogie Nights* had just come out, and Wahlberg was experiencing an endorphin rush as the glowing reviews and fawning interviewers made a trip to his Sunset Strip penthouse just below the Hollywood Hills seem like a trek up Mount Olympus.

But Wahlberg wasn't at home much these days. He was on the set in downscale downtown Culver City, a twenty-minute drive away from his Sunset aerie.

Every actor's and actress's dream is to work with Robert De Niro, and with *Out on My Feet*, Wahlberg would have his dream fulfilled. Plus *Out on My Feet* was a boxing movie, subject matter that had already won De Niro an Oscar for *Raging Bull*, a film that many critics consider the best ever made.

Like *Raging Bull*, *Out on My Feet* was based on a real-life boxer, Vinnie Curto, whose problems in and out of the ring make Mike Tyson's seem like Julie Andrews' psychohistory.

De Niro was to play legendary boxing trainer Angelo Dundee, the guiding light behind both Muhammad Ali, and the subject of this biopic, Vinnie Curto. The project must have had special resonance for the actor, since it represented his first return to the boxing ring since *Raging Bull.* The director, Barry Primus, wasn't nearly as accomplished as his star, but they had collaborated before on the lavishly praised but little-seen character drama, *Mistress* (1991).

Other behind-the-camera talent for the new movie included *Leaving Las Vegas'* production designer Waldemar Kalinowski, who knows how to sentimentalize sleaze beautifully, whether it's the tacky Las Vegas Strip or a punch-drunk pug's hole-in-the-wall apartment. The script was written by its subject, Vinnie Curto, then polished by veteran screenwriter Larry Golin. It must have been a hard piece of autobiography to pen. The story explores not only cruiserweight Curto's troubled ring career, but his horrifically abusive childhood as well.

For screenwriter Curto, however, the writing wasn't the most painful memory to relive. He also cast himself as his abusive father in the movie, reliving and reenacting traumatic memories perhaps better left unrecovered. *Out on My Feet* would be a real Rocky story, only Curto's demons were real, not on-screen foes like those played by Carl Weathers or Dolph Lundgren.

For Wahlberg, *Out on My Feet* would provide him with another chance to stretch artistically in a way he had never done before. Willing to transform himself into a fat cop in *The Corruptor*, for *Out on My Feet*, Wahlberg would have to trade ethnicities! The filmmakers were all prepared to turn the Irish Wahlberg into a young Italian Curto. Details of how this transformation would be made never surfaced, but a casting notice suggested that Wahlberg would definitely play ethnic, beginning with the search for youngsters to play Mark as a child.

An open casting call in *Drama-Logue* sought "Male: 6–12, Italian looking to play Mark Wahlberg as a child. Some boxing skills necessary." And "Male: 13–18, Italian looking to play Mark Wahlberg as an adolescent. Some boxing skills necessary."

As the adult Curto, brown-tinted contact lenses and hair dye were waiting in the wings to turn the Irish gangsta into an Italian stallion. Even Mark's idol, De Niro, had never been asked to transform himself into an Irishman. With *Out on My Feet*, Wahlberg would be invading Meryl Streep territory, a star who disappears into her role so thoroughly as to become unidentifiable on-screen.

For all its A-list talent, not to mention superagency CAA as the packager of the talent, *Out on My Feet* was a no-budget (by today's standards) independent film—a microscopic $9 million. Two days before principal photography was to begin on October 22, 1997, the production ran out of funds. The crew hadn't been paid in weeks, the production designer complained. "Every one of my crew feels robbed not only of money but of a great creative opportunity," Kalinowski said.

Director Primus said sadly, "I had confidence in the producers when we started out in April." Indeed, the director had been in pre-production with Curto for years. So had the producer, David B. Pritchard, who also headed the independent production company, Film Roman. Pritchard held off unpaid crew members for weeks with hopes of additional funding from a mysterious backer.

As the start date got closer, Pritchard desperately began to cut the budget in the hope of finding new backers. At one point, the project became so laughably no-budget, the producer's wife, Suzi Landolphi, donated her backyard sparring ring, which was transported to a soundstage in Culver City, a suburb of Los Angeles. (Landolphi's main business is a condom boutique on Melrose Avenue.)

Pritchard and Landolphi tried to rally the crew with a pep talk rather than paychecks. The couple compared their project to *The English Patient*, which also ran out of funds several times before going on to Academy Award Valhalla.

Production designer Kalinowski wasn't buying the analogy. "It made the crew furious. These are highly professional people with families to support, turning down other jobs, begging for favors from equipment houses and suppliers to make this work because of the low budget."

The fury of the crew expressed itself in grief and anger. Some crew members hurled paint on the sets they had lovingly built. Others broke down and cried. The film was to begin in October, and most of the crew members didn't have any jobs lined up for the rest of the year. They had hoped the production would last till Christmas. Then they would be able to afford to take time off for the holidays.

Pritchard apologized in the press, but he still seemed to be living with the hope that new financing was on the horizon. By that time, of course, it was too late since both De Niro and Wahlberg had left the project in disgust.

There's a sad photograph in the trades at this time that suggests what *Out on My Feet* might have been. From left to right, we see the very large director, Barry Primus, towering over the diminutive young man he has his arm around—Mark Wahlberg, in a baseball cap and button-down shirt. Wahlberg has his arm around an even smaller fellow, boxing trainer Angelo Dundee. At the end of this lineup stands another little guy, but a mountain when it comes to prestige and power, Robert De Niro. The principals had come together at Culver City to pose for publicity for a film that would never be produced, much less publicized.

A story still circulating, however, claims it wasn't lack of money that killed the project, but the *source* of the funding that eventually aborted it. In fact, according to this version, told to me by a good friend of Curto's and mine, there was plenty of funding available, but no one wanted to touch it. Least of all De Niro, who was always sensitive about his Italian roots and paranoid about contracting Frank Sinatra syndrome, guilt by association with the underworld.

This source told me that he believed the real reason the project collapsed was that Curto, still possessed by demons from his past, managed to turn off the rest of the cast and crew with his arrogance and belligerence. But what supposedly really did the project in was Curto's loud boasts about his unsavory business connections and their "affiliation" with the film. According to the source, when De Niro heard Curto's claims, he walked off the set in a panic, never to return. Financing for a film starring Robert De Niro easily could have been found elsewhere after the original backers balked. However, when De Niro left the project, the reason for making the film went with him. After *Boogie Nights*, Mark Wahlberg was hot, but De Niro's departure put a chill on the screen project, effectively killing it.

Daily Variety hinted at a less sinister reason for the film's demise: incompetence and lack of experience. The trade paper noted that little films tend to attract "inexperienced and ineffectual producers who think low-budget pics are a snap." *Variety* said that of the three producers (Steve Ecclesine, Stanton Dodson, and Stan Wakefield), only Wakefield had produced a feature film before, and most of his efforts were direct-to-video titles in the 1980s. Even more disturbing, the line producer (Steve Ecclesine), the person in charge of the day-to-day nuts and bolts of filmmaking, had never made a theatrical feature before.

What the movie producers lacked in experience, they tried to make up for with faith in the screen project. They put in their own money—$500,000—to keep the film afloat during five weeks of pre-production. The trades labeled that unprofessional as well.

Whatever the reasons the film stalled, some of the principals—but not De Niro and Wahlberg, who were too hot and busy to stick around while the money men played Monopoly with their careers—held out hope that *Out on My Feet* would eventually get up off the floor.

Producer Pritchard told the media, "I'm heartfully sorry for" the unpaid cast and crew, but added that new bank loans and overseas sales were potentially right around the corner. That was in October 1997. To date, the project remains on the back burner—or more accurately, in deep freeze.

Director Barry Primus didn't share his producer's optimism and called the project down for the count. He told the trade press, "Wonderful actors and crew members were drawn to this project, because it's an important story about a guy who is full of talent and promise but, because of childhood abuse, ends up destroying himself and those around him."

The subject of the movie and its co-author demonstrated the same pluckiness that had made him a contender until personal demons made his life story more suitable for a cautionary tale rather than a *Rocky*-style fairy tale. "I had my whole life and all my apples in this one. It's not gonna stop me," Curto, the former World Boxing Federation cruiserweight champ, insisted.

And after criticizing the producers' lack of experience and claiming they had "flirted with disaster," one reporter predicted *Out on My Feet* might find its legs after all. Plans to hustle the project at MIFED, the independent film fair held in Los Angeles every spring, might cobble together additional funds from overseas backers. And *Variety* reported that CAA, De Niro's agency, was actively trying to revive the moribund project, if for no other reason than to keep its most prestigious client happy.

To date, however, *Out on My Feet* remains in turnaround hell, and it's unlikely that super-hot, super-busy Wahlberg will ever return to the scene of this ring story, even if a backer comes forward with financing.

In the meantime, Mark kept himself busy with the action-adventure film *Three Kings,* about a group of soldiers who stumble upon a treasure during the Gulf War.

EPILOGUE AND PROLOGUE

Professional Highs, Personal Lows?

What do you get for the stud who has everything? How about a honey? Friends say Mark needs to find as brilliant a manager of his personal life as he has been a self-manager of his professional life. He's on record as a self-described lonely guy who wants a permanent squeeze.

With all his buds in residence, it's not exactly accurate to say it's lonely at the top floor of his apartment building overlooking the Sunset Strip. But he may be horny at the top. Friends paint a picture of Elvis-like isolation, complete with live-in entourage. Graceland in a highrise.

Visitors to both the Hollywood Hills home and the penthouse just south of it have commented on the absence of female guests, much less a girlfriend for Mark or any of his roommates.

"He doesn't like to have women just hanging out" at his penthouse, a friend who does hang out there told me. "It's pretty much a boys' club."

Wahlberg's brother Donnie once suggested Mark was holding out for something more substantial than T&A, maybe IQ. "There's only going to be so much tits and ass coming his way before he realizes that he wants a brain," Donnie said to the press.

One thing is clear. Groupies do not turn Mark on. In fact, any relationship with Mark has to be one of *mutual* adoration. "I'm not looking for a girl to throw herself at me. That's not the woman that I want to spend my life with. There has to be mutual respect, mutual love, mutual feelings. And the girl . . . I would have to be as quick to throw myself at her feet as she at mine," Mark said, amazingly introspective and not at all full of himself when he made that comment at the age of twenty-two.

After combing almost a decade of magazine and newspaper interviews, talking to close friends and business associates, and reading two books devoted to the star, I could only find published references to two women the actor expressed interest in. In January 1993, he grudgingly told *Entertainment Weekly* he was seeing a "Laurie" in New York. "She's someone I can hang out wit' and talk to. I know she's not tryin' to be around me because of who I am, because I knew her before."

A month later, *YM* magazine asked if Mark had a girlfriend, and he said simply, "No." Laurie had apparently already done a disappearing act.

In 1998, information on Wahlberg's love life was so hard to come by *Premiere* magazine resorted to quoting—at length—a Tarot-card reader, who advised Mark that an ex-girlfriend (unnamed, natch) would eventually resume the relationship, but Mark would have to fight to get her back. "You'll eventually succeed, "Joan" told him as she dealt his fate. "There are certain aspects to you that are pretty charming."

Wahlberg ordered the reporter from *Premiere* to "write that down, and tell her that I love her." However, when the journalist asked for the woman's name, Mark became coy. "Well, it's secret. But it's somebody that's been in my life."

Premiere's senior editor, Holly Millea, who conducted the interview, gave up her investigation and said resignedly, "It would take Kenneth Starr to get [his girlfriend's] ID."

His *Boogie Nights*' costar William H. Macy doubted if there even was one special woman. "I think Mark was breaking up with some girl every other week. Are you kidding? He's the luckiest guy who ever lived! And you know it doesn't hurt playing a character that's got the dick of death, either."

Mark doesn't lead a monkish existence. A mutual friend told me, "Every time he sees me, he wants me to fix him up with girls. I don't understand that because he can get girls."

The friend speculates that Mark engages in casual sex in Los Angeles because there's someone special back home in Massachusetts. "He calls her on his cell phone all the time," the friend said to me. He isn't "saving himself" for the woman back East, but he doesn't pursue other women seriously. "He does get laid here [in L.A.] all the time." The men who live with Mark brag about their conquests, although our mutual friend has never actually seen Mark on a date with a woman: "I don't see it! Seeing it is another thing." More often, the penthouse boys discuss their conquests *after* the fact.

The friend overhears Mark Wahlberg and his pal Mark Basile saying things like, "Hey, I just got a piece of ass the other day." They pick up women at clubs, the friend told me, although he's never seen them actually bring a woman to the penthouse for sex. Officially, though, Mark wants to settle down. "I'm a lonely person. Very lonely. I pray every day that a person will come along. I hope that there's one special person out there for me. I feel like I should already be married," he said in 1998.

The other object of Mark's desire is just a fantasy . . . and a pretty kinky one at that. A fan once asked him, "If you could go out with anyone, who would she be?"

Mark named movie star Sharon Stone, then modified his answer. The person he would really like to date is the character

(Catherine Tramell) Stone played in *Basic Instinct.* "I think it was just the movie *Basic Instinct* that moved me." Those who saw the number one box-office hit of 1992 will recall that Stone played a beautiful, immensely rich novelist with exquisite taste in clothes and interior decor. Oh, and she liked to kill men with an ice pick after tying them up with Hermés scarves and performing what Michael Douglas's character described as "the fuck of the century!"

If Mark is indeed lovelorn and fantasizes about making the ultimate snuff film with Ms. Tramell, at least he has his brother for company much of the time. When Donnie is on the West Coast making a movie, it's a case of "Su casa, mi penthouse"; i.e., Donnie lives with Mark and the boys. Unlike the rest of the fraternity, Donnie works regularly in film and TV projects.

A mutual friend told me, "Donnie isn't jealous of Mark's acting career because his is doing just fine, thank you very much!" Mark says there is no rivalry between brothers in the romance department, either. Maybe because there isn't a whole lot of romance, period. "Donnie used to get all the girls cuz he had the money. We got a lot of karma with girls. We generally like the same girls, but we never chase the same ones."

Donnie begs to differ and hints that as his show-business fame waned and Mark's waxed, the bigger star got the bigger—well, "amazing" experience. "The only time I was ever jealous of him was when he told me he went out with a girl who I thought was amazing and he told me she *was* amazing," Donnie said, sounding a bit envious.

Today, Mark Wahlberg says he regrets nothing he has done or experienced—his time in prison, his stage striptease, the bad-boy image. Asked if he could change anything in his past, he rejects the notion because all his experiences, even the nightmarish ones, have made him the person he is today. "I don't think that I would be the type of person that I am. I don't think that I would have the heart that I do."

Then he corrected himself. There is one thing he does regret. One person he's still making amends to is the long-suffering, belt-tightening Alma Wahlberg Conroy. "The only thing I'd do differently is to be a lot better to my mother. I would have kicked my other brothers' and sisters' asses for running my mother into the ground. My brothers and sisters ruined my mother's life, and I did too, through booze and then drugs and all that stuff.

"I thank my mother every day and apologize for not listening to her. She should have kicked me in the ass one more time! But everything else I would just let be."

A mutual friend of Mark's and mine says simply, "Mark *loves* his mom!" They talk on the phone every day, the friend told me.

Mark is bicoastal and divides his time evenly between his West Hollywood penthouse and Massachusetts, where he and Donnie still live in the Braintree mansion Donnie bought for his mother and stepfather. "Donnie and I have *always* lived with my mother," he tells the media.

Mark rarely mentions his real father in interviews, which led some fans to suspect an estrangement between the two following his parents' divorce in 1982. Mark put that speculation to rest when he revealed to the press that his father was battling cancer and heart disease. Donald Senior lives alone but gets plenty of visits from his son.

"The most I can do is spend as much time with him as possible. He's had a couple of strokes, so he's not in the best of health. Every time I see him, with his family, his grandchildren, he's the happiest guy in the world and the saddest at the same time.

"My dad never cried. Now he cries all the time. He took me to my first movies, and we still watch Cagney movies together."

According to Mark in comments to the media in recent years, his father is tremendously proud of Mark's success. "Oh, he loves it! He says, 'Who'd have ever thought it, Mikey?'" (Mark explained that he always wished he had been named Mikey, and his father obliges by calling him that.)

Donald Senior told him, "Kid, you made it. You're in the pictures. I always told you you should be in the pictures."

Mark responded, "Dad, you're in the pictures, too. I'm you."

My father, myself.

Superstars come and go, but mostly they go—into involuntary retirement, episodic TV, or, if they've made really bad investments, late-night infomercials, sharing a couch with a hair-care saleswoman or a Soloflex fetishist.

The box-office performance of his latest film, *The Big Hit*, suggests Mark won't be doing any late-night abdominal crunches anytime soon.

A single flop is never fatal once you've made it to the top of the charts. On average, it takes an entire decade of film failure before (a) you retire to the golf course, or (b) your luck turns and you stumble on to *The Nutty Professor* or *Pulp Fiction*.

With film projects stretching into the next millennium, Mark has at least until the year 2010 to tank, in his equivalent of *Waterworld* or *Last Action Hero.*

Fans of trivia may find the parallels and contrasts between the lives and careers of Matt Damon and Mark Wahlberg intriguing, if not eerie. The Germans have a term for how closely these two actors resemble one another: *doppelgänger*, which means a "ghostly double" who haunts a person.

Both men are in their late twenties and grew up in Boston. For his Oscar-nominated performance in *Good Will Hunting* (1997), it seems as though Damon practically borrowed Wahlberg's early life. Damon's Will Hunting sounds just like the bad boy Wahlberg was, even down to the geographical location and criminal record. Like the real-life Wahlberg, Hunting grew up on the mean streets of South Boston and has a rap sheet of assaults and robberies. Like Mark's days behind the wheel of a tow truck and in front of a masonry wall, trowel in hand, Hunting has a blue-collar job as a janitor at MIT. He's also a high-school dropout, just like Wahlberg, who has yet to earn his GED.

But that's as far as life imitates art in any comparisons between Damon and Wahlberg. Damon's real life, especially his formative years, couldn't have been more different from Wahlberg's. Damon's mother, Nancy Carlsson-Paige, is a professor of childhood education at Boston's Lesley College. Matt grew up in Cambridge, geographically not far from Dorchester, but light-years away, culturally. Damon's father, Kent, is a wealthy stockbroker. Unlike Mark, who was traumatized by his parents' split when he was eleven, Damon's parents divorced when he was only two, too young perhaps to experience the full devastation of divorce.

Although Damon convincingly played a juvenile delinquent in *Good Will Hunting*, in real life he seems more like *Leave It to Beaver*'s Eddie Haskell, the quintessential good boy. Damon's brother Kyle says, "We didn't rebel much. We didn't do drugs, stay out late or bad-mouth our parents." Compare this drug-free lifestyle with Wahlberg's indulgence in "wacky tobacky" and "secondhand" beer.

As Mark Wahlberg and Matt Damon grew older, the parallel lives which eventually led them to the same destination—the top of the Hollywood heap—diverged dramatically. Wahlberg dropped out of high school. Damon matriculated at Harvard, although he, too, would drop out, but only after spending three years at the most prestigious university in the nation.

During these formative years, both boys were devoted to writing; Damon to the script which won him an Oscar; Wahlberg, to rap lyrics which made him a multimillionaire.

Their filmography also reinforces the *doppelgänger* analogy. Mark played a supporting role as a heroin addict in *The Basketball Diaries.* Matt's character mainlined the same stuff in his first major role, *Courage Under Fire* (1996). Like Wahlberg, Damon was willing to trash his body for the sake of the role. Unlike Wahlberg, who blimped up for *The Corruptor,* Damon dropped forty pounds to play *Courage Under Fire*'s hollow-cheeked junkie.

Good Will Hunting was Damon's *Boogie Nights*, the film that catapulted him onto magazine covers, although he flew higher up into the firmament of stars than Wahlberg, since *Boogie Nights* was not a monster commercial success and failed to earn Wahlberg an Oscar.

These parallel lives further diverge in terms of film performance. Damon has the huge summer hit *Saving Private Ryan* (1998) under his belt and on his résumé, while Wahlberg has *The Big Hit*, without as big a box office, and certainly without the cachet of Steven Spielberg behind the camera. At least Wahlberg can point to his association with another class act, Oliver Stone, the producer of *The Corruptor*.

Any comparisons between the two actors which praise Matt at Mark's expense are inherently invidious: Damon was born with the geographical and parental equivalent of a silver spoon in his mouth. Wahlberg ate "hand-me-downs," the school lunches appropriated by his father.

Although Mark Wahlberg has managed his past brilliantly, he does not obsess about the future—at least not his professional future. We'll leave romance and twelve-step meetings for discussions with a therapist or better yet, one of our mutual confidants.

From his penthouse perch, Mark Robert Michael Wahlberg views things with an appropriately Olympian detachment. And well-deserved satisfaction for a job that continues to be well—hell!—magnificently done.

As Wahlberg confided to the press not long ago, "The thing with me is, though, I'm not out to prove anything to anybody other than myself. I've had a huge amount of success and I'd like to make wonderful movies for the rest of my life. If not, hey, growing up where I came from, I've done more than I ever thought I would have accomplished."

FEATURE FILMS

Renaissance Man

(1994, a Touchstone Pictures release)

CREDITS: Executive producers, Penny Marshall, Buzz Feitshans; producers, Sara Colleton, Elliot Abbott, Robert Greenhut; co-producers, Timothy M. Bourne, Amy Lemisch; director, Penny Marshall; screenplay, Jim Burnstein; camera, Adam Greenberg; editors, George Bowers, Battle Davis; music, Hans Zimmer; production designer, Geoffrey Kirkland; art director, Richard L. Johnson; costumes, Betsy Heimann; sound, Les Lazarowitz; casting, Paula Herold. Rating, PG-13; running time, 129 minutes; released June 3, 1994.

CAST: Danny DeVito (Bill Rago); Gregory Hines (Sergeant Cass); Cliff Robertson (Colonel James); James Remar (Captain Murdoch); Lillo Brancato Jr. (Donnie Benitez); Stacey Dash (Private Miranda Myers); Ed Begley Jr. (Jack Markin); Kadeem Hardison (Private Jamaal Montgomery); Mark Wahlberg (Tommy Lee Haywood); Gary Dewitt Marshall (Traffic M.P.); Ben Wright (Private Oswald); Jenifer Lewis (Mrs. Coleman).

The Basketball Diaries

(1995, a New Line Cinema release)

CREDITS: Executive producers, Chris Blackwell, Dan Genetti; producers, Liz Heller, John Bard Manulis; director, Scott Kalvert; screenplay, Bryan Goluboff, based on the memoir by Jim Carroll; camera, David Phillips; editor, Dana Congdon; music, Graeme Revell; production designer, Christopher Nowak; set decorator, Harriet Zucker; costumes, David C. Robinson; sound, Paul Clay, William Sarokin; casting, Avy Kaufman. Rating, R; running time, 102 minutes; released April 21, 1995.

CAST: Leonardo DiCaprio (Jim Carroll); Bruno Kirby (Swifty); Lorraine Bracco (Jim's mother); Ernie Hudson (Reggie); Patrick McGaw (Neutron); James Madio (Pedro); Mark Wahlberg (Mickey); Juliette Lewis (Diane Moody); Roy Cooper (Father McNulty); Toby Huss (Kenny); Michael Imperioli (Bobby); Manny Alfaro (Manny); Jim Carroll (Frankie Pinewater); Marilyn Sokol (Chanting Woman) Josh Mostel (Counterman); Michael Rapaport (Skinhead); John Hoyt (Billy the Bartender); Barton Heyman (Confessional Priest).

Fear

(1996, a Universal Release of an
Imagine Entertainment presentation)

CREDITS: Executive producer, Karen Kehela; producers, Brian Grazer, Ric Kidney; director, James Foley; screenplay, Christopher Crowe; camera, Thomas Kloss; editor, David Brenner; music, Carter Burwell; music supervision, Danny Bramson; production designer, Alex McDowell; art direction, Richard Hudolin; set decoration, D. Fauquet-Lemaitre; costumes, Kirsten Everberg; sound, Eri J. Batut; associate producer, Karen Snow. Rating, R; running time, 96 minutes; released April 22, 1996.

CAST: Mark Wahlberg (David McCall); Reese Witherspoon (Nicole Walker); William Petersen (Steve Walker); Amy Brenneman (Laura Walker); Alyssa Milano (Margo Masse); Christopher Gray (Toby); Todd Caldecott (Gary Rohmer); Tracy Fraim (Logan); Gary John Riley (Hacker).

Traveller

(1997, an October Films release)

CREDITS: Executive producers, Robert Mickelson, Rick King; producers, Bill Paxton, Brian Swardstrom, Mickey Liddell, David Blocker; director, Jack Green; screenplay, Jim McGlynn; camera, Jack N. Green; editor, Michael Ruscio; music, Andy Paley; production designer, Michael Helmy; set decoration, Steve Davis; costumes, Douglas Hall; sound, Carl Rudisill; casting; Joseph Middleton. Rating, R; running time, 100 minutes; released April 18, 1997.

CAST: Bill Paxton, (Bokky Sherlock); Mark Wahlberg (Pat O'Hara); Julianna Margulies (Jean Gentry); James Gammon (Double D); Luke Askew (Boss Jack Costello); Nikki Deloach (Kate); Michael Shaner (Lip); Robert Peters (Farmer's Son); Danielle Wiener (Shane).

Boogie Nights

(1997, a New Line Cinema release)

CREDITS: Executive producer, Lawrence Gordon; producers, Lloyd Levin, John Lyons, Paul Thomas Anderson, Joanne Sellar; director, Paul Thomas Anderson; screenplay, Paul Thomas Anderson; camera, Robert Elswit; editor; Dylan Tichenor; music, Michael Penn; production designer, Bob Ziembicki; set decoration, Sandy Struth; costumes, Mark Bridges; sound, Stephen Halbert; casting, Christine Sheaks. Rating, R; running time, 152 minutes; released, October 20, 1997.

CAST: Mark Wahlberg (Eddie Adams/Dirk Diggler); Burt Reynolds (Jack Horner); Julianne Moore (Amber Waves); John C. Reilly (Reed Rotchild);

Don Cheadle (Buck Swope); Heather Graham (Rollergirl); Luis Guzman (Maurice T. Rodriguez); Phillip Seymour Hoffman (Scotty); William H. Macy (Little Bill); Alfred Molina (Rahad Jackson); Phillip Baker Hall (Floyd Gondolli); Robert Ridgely (The Colonel).

The Big Hit

(1998, a TriStar Pictures presentation)

CREDITS: Executive producers, John Woo, Terence Chang, John M. Eckert; producers, Warren Zide, Wesley Snipes; co-producers, Craig Perry, Victor McGauley, Roger Garcia; director, Che-Kirk Wong; screenplay, Ben Ramsey; camera, Danny Nowak; editors, Robin Russell, Pietro Scalia; music, Graeme Revell; production designer, Taavo Soodor; set decoration, Enrico Campana; costumes, Margaret Mohr; sound, Douglas Ganton; casting, Roger Mussenden. Rating, R; running time, 93 minutes; released April 24, 1998.

CAST: Mark Wahlberg (Melvin Smiley); Lou Diamond Phillips (Cisco); Christina Applegate (Pam Shulman); Avery Brooks (Paris); Bokeem Woodbine (Crunch); Cina Chow (Keiko Nishi); Antonio Sabato Jr. (Vince); Lainie Kazan (Jeanne Shulman); Elliott Gould (Morton Shulman); Sab Shimono (Jiro Nishi); Robin Dunne (Gump); Lela Rochon (Chantel); Danny Smith (Video Store Kid); Joshua Peace (Lance); David Usher (Sergio).

Forthcoming Releases

The Corruptor

(1999, a New Line Cinema release)

CREDITS: Executive producer, Bill Carraro; producers, Oliver Stone, Dan Halsted; co-producer, John Krauss; director, James Foley; screenplay, Robert Pucci; camera, Juan Ruiz-Anchia; editor, Howard Smith; production designer, David Brisbin; art director, Paul Austerberry; set decorator, Jaro Dick; sound, Douglas Ganton; casting, Mary Vernineur.

CAST: Mark Wahlberg (Danny Wallace); Chow Yun-Fat (Nick Chen); Elizabeth Lindsey (Louise Deng); Byron Mann (Bobby Vu); Ric Young (Henry Lee).

The Yards

(1999, a Miramax release)

CREDITS: Producers, Paul Webster, Nick Wechsler, Kerry Orent; co-producer, Christopher Goode; director, James Gray; screenplay, James Gray; camera, Harris Savides; editor, Jeff Ford; production designer, Kevin Thompson; art director, Judy Rhee; set decorator Ford wheeler; costumes, Michael Clancy; sound, Tom Paul; casting, Doug Aibel.

CAST: Mark Wahlberg (Leo Handler); Joaquin Phoenix (Willie Gutierrez); Charlize Theron (Erica Olchin); James Caan (Frank Olchin); Ellen Burstyn (Val Handler); Faye Dunaway (Kitty Olchin).

TELEVISION FILMS

The Substitute

(1993, USA Cable)

CREDITS: Executive producer, David Kirkpatrick; producer, Matthew O'Connor; director, Martin Donovan; screenplay, Cynthia Verlaine; camera, Glen MacPherson; music, Gerald Gouriet; set decorator, Berry Kemp. Rating, R; aired running time: 100 minutes; aired September 22, 1993.

CAST: Amanda Donohoe (Gayle Richardson/Laura Ellington), Dalton James (Josh Wyatt); Natasha Gregson Wagner (Jenny); Eugene Robert Glazer (Ben Wyatt); Mark Wahlberg (Ryan Westerberg); Pat Bermel (Frank); Lossen Chambers (Kim); David Frankham (Riggs); Fran Gebhard (Female Teacher); Cusse Mankuma (Bernard); D. Neil Mark (Rusty); Martin Martinuzzi (Doug Richards); Molly Parker (Courtney); Justine Priestley (Claire Bilino); Christian Svensson (Dave Korczuk).

CDs

Marky Mark and The Funky Bunch, Music for the People

(1991, Atlantic/Interscope Records [catalog number: 91737])
Executive producer, Marc Benesch; producer/arranger, Donnie Wahlberg.

TRACKS: Music for the People, Good Vibrations, Wildside, 'Bout Time I Funk You, Peace, So What Chu Sayin', Marky Mark Is Here, On the House Trip, Make Me Say Ooh!, I Need Money, The Last Song on Side B.

SINGLES: Good Vibrations, Wildside, I Need Money, Peace.

LONG-FORM VIDEO: Marky Mark and The Funky Bunch, *Music for the People* (1991)

Marky Mark and The Funky Bunch, You Gotta Believe

(1992, Atlantic/Interscope Records [catalog number: 92203])
Executive producer, Marc Benesch; producer/arranger, Donnie Wahlberg.

TRACKS: Intro: The Crisis, You Gotta Believe, Gonna Have a Good Time, Loungin' [featuring Donnie D], Don't Ya Sleep, I Want You, The American Dream [featuring Donnie D], The "M," Get UP (The Funky Bunch Theme), Super Cool Mack Daddy, I Run Rhymes, Ain't No Stopping the Funky Bunch, The Last Song On Side B, Part II: Go On, The Solution.

SINGLE: You Gotta Believe.

VIDEO

The Marky Mark Workout: Form, Focus, Fitness

(1993, a Good Times Home Video release
[catalog number: 0579319])

CREDITS: Executive producers, Mark Wahlberg, Andrew Greenberg; executive in charge of production, Ernest Schultz; director, Scott Kalvert; camera, David Phillips; exercise program developed by John Alves, Rich Minzer; nutritional program developed by Neal Spruce; music producer/composer, Donnie Wahlberg for Donnie D. Productions; running time, 70 minutes.

BIBLIOGRAPHY

Books

Catalano, Grace. *New Kids on the Block*. New York: Bantam, 1990.

Erlewine, Michael, Vladimir Bogdanov, Chris Woodstra, Stephen Thomas Erlewine, and Richie Unterberger (editors). *All Music Guide to Rock: The Experts' Guide to the Best Rock, Pop, Soul, R&B and Rap*. San Francisco: Miller Freeman Books, 1997.

Marky Mark and Lynn Goldsmith. *Marky Mark*. New York: HarperPerennial, 1992.

Matthews, Jill. *The Lives and Loves of New Kids on the Block*. NewYork: Pocket Books, 1990.

Perkins, William Eric (editor). *Droppin' Science: Critical Essays on Rap Music and Hip-Hop Culture*. Philadelphia: Temple University Press, 1996.

Potter, Russell A. *Spectacular Vernaculars: Hip-Hop and the Politics of Postmodernism*. New York: State University of New York Press, 1995.

Reisfeld, Randi. *Marky Mark and the Funky Bunch*. New York: Avon Books, 1992.

Ro, Ronin. *Gangsta: Merchandising the Rhymes of Violence*. New York: St. Martin's Press, 1996.

Rose, Tricia. *Rap Music and Black Culture in Contemporary America*. Connecticut: Wesleyan University Press, 1994.

Small, Michael, and Al Pereira. *Break It Down: The Inside Story from the New Leaders of Rap*. New York: Citadel Press, 1992.

Magazines, Newspapers, and Other Periodicals

Abele, Robert. "1998 Breakthrough Awards." *US*, April 1998, p. 71.

Anketell, Michael. "Behind the Briefs." *POZ*, November 1996, pp. 7–79, 95, 112.

Ansen, David. "Porn in the U.S.A." *Newsweek*, October 6, 1997, pp. 74–75.

Ascher-Walsh, Rebecca. "Boogie Night." *Entertainment Weekly*, March 6, 1998, pp. 41–42.

Brasel, Dale. *Details* (cover story), May 1997.

Bruni, Frank. "Reconstructing Marky Mark." *New York Times Magazine*, August 31, 1997, pp. 26, 28.

Cohen, Debi. "Marky Mark Exposed." *YM,* February 1993, pp. 39ff.

Colapinto, John. "Missing: White Rapper. Last Seen Wearing Calvin Klein Underwear." *US,* July 1993, pp. 31ff.

Davis, Ivor. "The Naked Truth About Mark Wahlberg." *New York Times* Syndicate, November 1997.

Details. "The 1998 *Details* Movie Awards." March 1998.

Farley, Christopher John. "Marky Mark's New." *Time*, October 6, 1997, pp. 86, 88.

Hedegaard, Erik. "Marquee Mark." *Details*, April 1996, pp. 117ff.

Hedegaard, Erik. "The X-Rated Redemption of Mark Wahlberg." *Rolling Stone*, October 30, 1997.

Hendrickson, Matt. "Random Notes." *Rolling Stone*, April 2, 1998, p. 16.

Karger, Dave. "Next of Skin." *Entertainment Weekly,* July 19, 1996, p. 57.

Kenny, Glenn. "Making It." *Premiere,* September 1997, pp. 78–79.

Klady, Leonard. "Top 250 of 1997." *Daily Variety*, March 9, 1998.

Levy, Emmanuel. *Boogie Nights* film review. *Variety*, September 15, 1997, p. 68.

Leyva, Ric. "The Journey from Marky Mark to *Boogie Nights*." Associated Press/*Daily News* (Los Angeles), November 5, 1997, p. 7.

Merkin, Daphne. "The Skin Game." *New Yorker*, October 13, 1997, pp. 97–98.

Mooney, Joshua. "*Boogie Nights* Goes Beyond Marky Mark." Entertainment News Wire, October 19, 1997.

Pareles, Jon. "At Lunch with Marky Mark." *New York Times,* April 8, 1992.

Pearce, Garth. "Marky Mark Finally Makes His Mark." London *Sunday Times*, January 11, 1998.

Rebello, Stephen. "The Boogie Man." *Movieline*, June 1997, pp. 57–60, 86–87.

Rozen, Leah. *Boogie Nights* film review. *People*, October 20, 1997, p. 21.

Schwarzbaum, Lisa. "Boy Toy." *Entertainment Weekly,* January 15, 1993, pp. 19ff.

Sischy, Ingrid. "The Mark'd Man." *Interview,* October 1997, pp. 121–22.

Smith, Gavin. "Night Fever." *Sight and Sound*, January 1998, pp. 7–10, 36–37.

Thompson, Malissa. "Cause Celeb: Undie Achievers." *Premiere*, September 1993.

Travers, Peter. "Boogie Nights." *US*, November 1997, p. 55.

Trebay, Guy. "Heather Graham Was the Honey in *Boogie Nights* . . ." *Details*, March 1998, pp. 161, 215.

Wayne, George. "Porn to Be Wild." *Vanity Fair*, August 1997.

Wieder, Judy. "His Turn." *The Advocate*, January 25, 1994, pp. 61, 63, 68–74.

Williams, Linda Ruth. *Boogie Nights* film review. *Sight and Sound*, January 1998, pp. 36–37.

Sources of Chapter Opening Quotes

Epigraph— Marky Mark and Lynn Goldsmith, *Marky Mark*. New York: HarperPerennial, 1992.

Jan Stuart, "Mark on Mark: Naked Truth," *Los Angeles Times*, November 1, 1997, p. F-13.

Introduction—Ron Givens. "Hanging Buff." *New York Daily News*, April 12, 1998, p.14.

Chapter 1—Ingrid Sischy. "The Mark'd Man." *Interview*, October 1997, p. 122.

Chapters 15 and 17—Matt Hendrickson, "Random Notes," *Rolling Stone*, April 2, 1998, p. 16.

INDEX

ABOUT THE AUTHOR

Frank Sanello is the author of biographies on Tom Cruise, Steven Spielberg, Sharon Stone, Jimmy Stewart, Will Smith, and the current bestseller, *Eddie Murphy: The Life and Times of a Comic on the Edge.*

As a journalist for the past twenty-five years, Sanello has written for the *Washington Post*, the *Chicago Tribune*, the *New York Times* Syndicate, and *People, Cosmopolitan,* and *Penthouse* magazines. He was also the film critic for the *Los Angeles Daily News* and a business reporter for UPI.

A native of Joliet, Illinois, Sanello graduated from the University of Chicago with honors and earned a master's degree from UCLA's film school. A purple belt in Tae Kwon Do, Sanello volunteers as a kickboxing instructor at AIDS Project Los Angeles.

The author recently completed a biography of Sylvester Stallone, *A Rocky Life*. A man of wide-ranging interests, Sanello is currently writing a history of nineteenth-century China's opium wars with Britain.

Sanello lives in West Hollywood, California, with one bossy dog and four nervous cats.

Also available from
Renaissance Books

Matt Damon: The Unauthorized Biography
by Chris Nickson
ISBN: 1-58063-072-3 • $16.95

That Lawyer Girl: The Unauthorized Guide to Ally's World
by A. C. Beck
ISBN: 1-58063-044-8 • $14.95

The Girl's Got Bite: An Unofficial Guide to Buffy's World
by Kathleen Tracy
ISBN: 1-58063-035-9 • $14.95

Party of Five: The Unofficial Companion
by Brenda Scott Royce
ISBN: 1-58063-000-6 • $14.95

Hercules & Xena: The Unofficial Companion
by James Van Hise
ISBN: 1-58063-001-4 • $15.95

Pufnstuf & Other Stuff
The Weird and Wonderful World of Sid & Marty Krofft
by David Martindale, foreword by Marty Krofft &
afterword by Sid Krofft
ISBN: 1-58063-007-3 • $16.95

The Ultimate Marilyn
by Ernest W. Cunningham
ISBN: 1-58063-003-0 • $16.95

The Ultimate Barbra
by Ernest W. Cunningham
ISBN: 1-58063-041-3 • $16.95

To order please call
1-800-452-5589